Children Solve Problems

Children Solve
Problems
Edward de Bono

Harper & Row, Publishers

New York, Evanston
San Francisco, London

FIRST U.S. EDITION 1974

Library of Congress Cataloging in Publication Data

De Bono, Edward, 1933–
    Children solve problems.
    1. Problem solving (Child psychology) I. Title.
BF723.P8D43   1974   155.4'13'0207   73-5459
ISBN 0-06-011024-4

Contents

Preface

Almost all the drawings in this book were obtained in the course
of a design project which I ran in the educational journal *Where*,
which is published by the Advisory Centre for Education. I am very
grateful to Beryl McAlhone, the editor of *Where*, for her cooperation
in running the design project. At that time there was no intention
of publishing the drawings in any other way. It was at the
suggestion of Martin Lightfoot of Penguin Education that the
drawings were put together in a more complete way in this book.
I myself agree that the drawings are so good that they deserve this
further publication.

The drawings showing improvements in the design of the human body
were obtained from Sawston Junior School through the help of David
Johns and his staff. I am very grateful to Audrey Davies who
transcribed a very hurried tape recording into this book.

I would like to take this new opportunity to thank all those
teachers and parents who sent in designs for the original series in
Where. Since there are thousands of designs, it has never been
possible for me to thank them as personally as they deserve. It is
always encouraging to be reminded that there really are teachers
who are enthusiastic and who do care. Unfortunately, even in this
book it is only possible to use a fraction of the drawings sent in.
They are not necessarily the best ones, but simply the ones that
can be most easily reproduced. For instance, very detailed drawings
and coloured drawings were not suitable.

The proceeds from this book go to the Cognitive Research Trust,
which is concerned with the study of thinking, and which is
working towards the point when it might have enough funds to
carry out a research programme in this important but largely
neglected area.

Introduction

We can learn a lot from children, and especially from watching children think. Children can be brilliant thinkers. When children were given the 'political' problem of stopping a cat and a dog from fighting their ideas went far beyond the approaches used by politicians. It is not that we judge children with indulgence; they are genuinely more fluent with ideas. It is this fluency that gives children an advantage over adults in creativity and lateral thinking. On several occasions I have asked a lecture hall full of highly-educated and highly-paid thinking men to design a dog-exercising machine. They take the request in good humour but the ideas produced are nothing like as good as those produced by children. From time to time every creative person wishes he had the outlook of a child so that he could find his own perceptions and escape from the ones that have been imposed on him. This book is intended to provide an opportunity to look directly at the thinking of children.

A child enjoys thinking. He enjoys the use of his mind just as he enjoys the use of his body as he slides down a helter skelter or bounces on a trampoline. This enjoyment is reflected in the following comments which came in just some of the covering letters with children's designs:

Too late I suppose! But the children concerned so enjoyed doing them that I didn't have the heart not to send them. (Know College, Jamaica)

The enclosed was completed in a high state of excitement within half an hour of my suggesting to Philip that he 'had a go'.

They obviously enjoyed doing this. The younger one kept happy for quite a while and the elder one finished his design in twenty minutes.

I am now sending you some of the inventions designed by my class of nine year olds. They thoroughly enjoyed this and we are having an inventions corner to display the other designs they thought up.

They enjoyed doing them enormously.

In going through this book I hope you will be as impressed as I always am by the sheer ability of young children to think. At first sight the drawings may appear to be no more than cute, crazy and amusing, but if you study them more closely and put yourself into the position of the child you will suddenly appreciate the thinking involved in each case. A child's knowledge and experience are limited and so the problem solutions are often impractical. But what matters is the way the child's mind uses the limited material at its disposal.

If children can already think so well at this age, then surely the long years of education must develop this ability to a high level. Not so. At the end of education there has been no improvement in the thinking ability of children – in fact there has actually been a deterioration. This opinion is based on experiments involving several thousand people all of whom had benefited from higher education. It is an opinion which seems to be shared by others who have considered the matter. Why should education have this effect on thinking ability?

Education has always regarded its prime duty to be transfer of knowledge and those who have doubted the wisdom of this approach have usually been brought to their senses by the practical responsibilities of examinations. In transferring knowledge teachers are keenly aware that the only valid criterion of success is for the pupils' output to match the teacher's input. Although the extreme example of this – the example of rote learning – is dying out (more slowly than many imagine) the emphasis is still on doing things 'as they should be done'. This emphasis not only makes it unnecessary to think, but is also dangerous for the unfortunate pupil who comes up with an unacceptable, new point of view. To be fair it should perhaps be added that this method of transferring knowledge is sometimes quite effective if that is what you want to achieve, but the knowledge may not outlast the exams for which it is stored.

The amount of knowledge that has to be transferred is increasing all the time and as a result the student today has much less time to think than ever before. It is true that in some specialized areas, and in passing exams, knowledge is more useful than the ability to think but it may be of little use outside those areas or in helping a person to live with himself and with society. The emphasis on orthodoxy and the amount of knowledge required inhibit the development of thinking ability but may nevertheless be necessary with the education system as it is at the moment. What is worse is that no time is deliberately set aside for the encouragement of thinking ability. If thinking ability were being actively encouraged in one oasis area then its neglect in other areas would not matter so much. The absence of any such direct attention to thinking is to my mind the main cause of the deterioration of thinking ability during education.

The idea that thinking can be treated as a learnable skill is already taken for granted in two other areas of human activity. These are the business world and the computer world, both of which have to deal with reality, unlike the self-satisfying world of education which measures its own success for itself. In business poor thinking means bankruptcy and in the computer world it means a waste of expensive computer time. In education, alas, it is undetectable. For some time now the business world has been paying direct attention to such aspects of thinking as decision-making, planning, innovation and problem-solving and treating them as learnable skills. From the computer world comes the idea of 'heuristics', which includes all those aspects of thinking which cannot be fitted into mathematical formulations. The paradox is that it required the logical efficiency of the computer to demonstrate that logic is only part of thinking. In the computer world increasing attention is being paid to the thinking that has to take place before a situation is parcelled up into neat concepts that can be worked on with logic. This switch from logical thinking to what might be called perceptual or lateral thinking is a much more important change in thinking about thinking than most people in education realize. Most of them continue to assume that sufficient excellence in logic is all that is required in thinking.

I have often been told that there are four sorts of people in education: fools, knaves, the passive and the impatient. I have met several of the impatient ones but it is clear that they do not run the system and indeed they soon get edged out. As to the other categories I believe that there are not many fools and knaves though they may have an effect out of proportion to their numbers. The majority fall into the passive bracket – not because they are passive in themselves but because the self-preserving character of the education system is so strong as to make them despair of the usefulness of activity. It has been said that education serves two functions supremely well: it preserves its own jobs and it keeps children out of the home. The reaction of most teachers to the idea of teaching thinking as a specific subject is not a negative one. On the contrary, they are enthusiastic about it but are doubtful about how it can be done.

There would be very little problem in developing and testing a method of teaching thinking directly as a specific subject in its own right. I have already started a project (TAP: Thinking-Ability Project) whereby teachers in different schools try out various formats for the teaching of thinking. It is not a question of creating a body of dogma that has to be learned (like geometry) but of creating special situations which develop thinking ability directly because they are learning situations. The situations do have to be carefully structured so that students can learn from each other, for if the situations are loose the students are working on projects so different that this important aspect of learning is lost. Principles, strategies, guidelines, awareness of error, are all fed in along with the direct-thinking experience. Since the impetus to carry out such a project is unlikely to come from the educational establishment – which is too tied up in the administration of education to be concerned about its content – there is a need for some foundation to take the lead. The importance of the subject and the rewards are great – but so is the boldness required. But when thinking is finally part of the curriculum I believe we shall look back and wonder why it ever seemed a strange idea.

In this book children are shown solving a variety of problems. Problem-solving may seem to be a rather specialized part of thinking. But if we change the name to 'dealing with a situation', 'overcoming an obstacle', 'bringing about a desired effect', 'making something happen', then it can be seen that the thinking involved is very much the thinking that is involved in everyday life even though the actual problems may appear exotic. The convenience of problem-solving as one format for practising thinking is that there is a defined objective. Problem-solving is by no means the whole of thinking but the processes are not essentially different from other thinking processes and it is a convenient way of demonstrating these processes. (In spite of this, not everyone in education has had much to do with thinking. One educational journalist for instance declared himself unable to see what designing a dog-exercising machine had to do with thinking.)

Each of the problems in this book was chosen because it has some special feature. The cat-and-dog problem is a political problem involving psychology and motivation. The elephant problem involves dealing with magnitude and also dealing with matters well outside personal experience. The house-building problem involves making an existing complex process faster and more efficient. The fun machine involves choice and direct experience. The policeman-and-bad-man problem involves moral judgements. And so on.

Finally, a word about drawings. Many people ask me why I seem to prefer drawings to words as a thinking medium for children. There are several reasons. Young children are not always very good at expressing their ideas in words and it would be a pity if their ideas were to be restricted by insisting that they use words. Again, words can sometimes be difficult to understand and interpreting the meaning behind them may become a matter of guesswork. Drawings, however, are clear and relatively unambiguous. To make a drawing you have to commit yourself to a definite idea: you cannot say 'the bricks are put in position more quickly than usual' in a drawing because you have to show exactly how this is done. There are more advantages. With a drawing the whole idea is visible all at once and you can work at it with addition, alteration, modification, change, etc. With words you have either to remember it all in your mind or else read through your description each time you want to see what you have got. It is significant that in a recent survey of inventive people the only uniform characteristic was their use of drawings and sketches in their thinking. Finally, there is the fact that children from disadvantaged backgrounds are often handicapped when it comes to the use of words. But preliminary work suggests that there is no such handicap with visual expression.

To my mind it is a waste of time to flip through this book making 'how cute!' exclamations before moving on to the next drawing. The more you look at a drawing the more you will find in it. Each drawing is a laboratory in which to study. The study of how children think is the best basis for *understanding* how children think. This is obvious. But what is less obvious is that such a study is also a very good basis for understanding how adults think. The differences between the way children think and the way adults do it is much smaller than most adults believe.

Children Solve Problems

1 Stop a Cat and a Dog Fighting

Show how you would stop a cat and a dog from fighting.

This is *the basic* political problem. How to stop people with differences from fighting each other. The differences may be racial, religious, ideological, or based on nationality. Cats and dogs are as racially and culturally different as any two human groups, and traditionally they are supposed to be always fighting each other.

The starting situation is very definite – there are cats and dogs which are distinct and which fight each other. The objective is also very definite – how to stop them fighting. What means would children use to try to achieve this objective? Would they take into account the psychology of a cat and a dog, or would they try and use purely physical means? Even if they used physical means, these could only work in the end if they had psychological effects. As there are no traditional, stereotyped ways of stopping a cat and a dog from fighting, the children would have to solve the problem on their own. They would have to come up with their own ideas of how to stop the fight.

How practical would the children's ideas on fight-stopping be? Would these ideas reflect the political thinking that adults have tried throughout the ages, or would they show different approaches. The language and the ideas used by children might be simple because they have to fit in with the limited experience of a child. And yet the principles involved may themselves be very sophisticated: all one needs to do is to change the names a little to find that they may apply directly in adult political thinking.

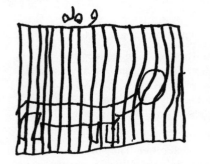 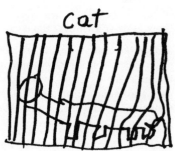

Cat and dog – 1

The ghetto concept. The
traditional way of stopping two
different groups from fighting
is to put them in separate cages
or within national boundaries
and keep them apart. In this way
they cannot get at each other
to fight. It does not always work,
especially when the two groups
cannot be separated in this way.

Cat and dog - 2

A variation on the ghetto concept. The cages here are balls and
chains which restrict free movement. For instance, the need for
visas, special passports and so on, which achieve the same effect
as a cage-type or wall-type ghetto.

Cat and dog – 3

An ingenious idea which constitutes an automatic ghetto. The
slippery material on the feet of the dogs and cats presumably
would not inconvenience them in general, but as soon as they start
to fight then they slip apart and are unable to get at each other's
throat. Certainly worth considering in its political implications.

Put a very strong see through wall beteen the cat and the dogs feeding ~~placein~~ places so they can see eachother but they ~~can not~~ can not fight. Later take it away

Cat and dog – 4

The arm's length concept. The cat and the dog are not completely separated but held at arm's length so that they cannot get at each other's throat. But they can see each other very clearly and get used to each other, and in the end they may come to love each other. Probably does not work because the more you see of your enemy perhaps the more you get to hate him. Optimistic!

Cat and dog – 5

A variation of the arm's length concept. This time there is no
physical barrier but the two have a certain range of movement
and can get quite close to each other but not really close enough
to fight.

Cat and dog - 6

Another variation of the arm's length concept with the cat and
dog each at the end of an arm. They can circle round and round a
track and go past each other's home, where there is in each case
a jar of scent to 'scare' the cat or dog. Thus they can get used to
each other's home ground without ever being allowed to get close
enough to fight. Note that individually both of them are well
looked after. For instance there are individual hutches in case
either of them gets tired. Each is also protected from the weather
by an umbrella. Two special hands are provided, one in case the
dog bites and the other in case the cat spits. These are additional
protection.

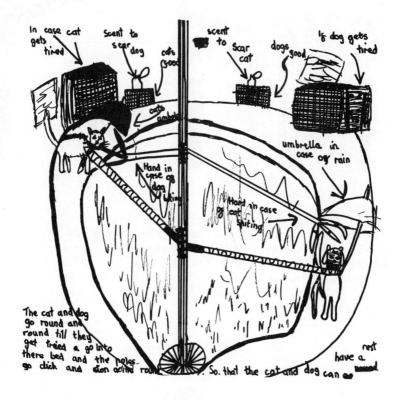

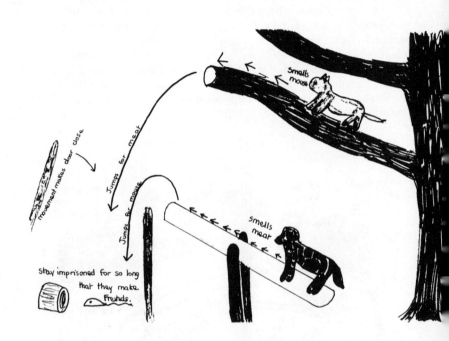

Smells mouse

Jumps for meat

movement makes door close

Jumps for mouse

smells meat

Stay imprisoned for so long that they make Friends.

Cat and dog - 7

The exact opposite of the ghetto concept. This could be called the 'let them get on with it' concept. The cat and the dog are separately tricked into jumping into the same enclosure. Their movement in entering the enclosure makes the lid come down very firmly. And then they are left to get on with it, and to fight it out or get used to each other.

first of all   I put them in cages and then
talk to them   and I   say," Now Dog, you're going
to meet   a cat", and " Now Cat, you're going
to meet   a dog". And I get them out on a
nice   sunny day, both together, and what I
do is,   I have   a   game of ball with them.

Cat and dog - 8

The distraction concept. Athletics stop all fights. The cat and the
dog are kept in their separate ghetto cages, and then they are
brought out on a nice sunny day to play ball together (Olympic
Games). So they make friends and live in peace happily ever after.

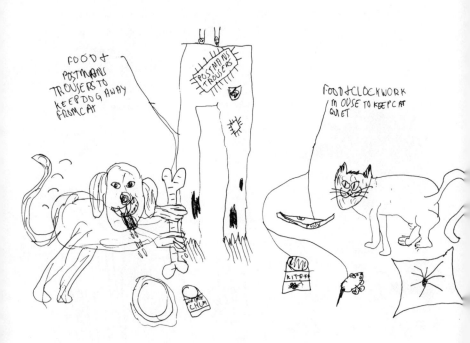

FOOD+ POSTMANS TROUSERS TO KEEP DOG AWAY FROM CAT

POSTMANS TROUSERS

POSTMANS TROUSERS

FOOD+CLOCKWORK MOUSE TO KEEP CAT QUIET

CHUM

KIT-E-KAT

Cat and dog – 9

An extension of the distraction concept. Keep both cat and dog happy and they will have no time to fight each other. To keep the (Edward Heath-looking) dog happy, all you have to do is to provide a bone for him to chew, a tin of Pedigree Chum and a pair of postman's trousers for him to worry. The cat is kept happy with a tin of Kit-e-Kat, a clockwork mouse and a cushion to sit on.

You tie a Fish to the cats tail and a steak to dogs, and by the time the have finished running round in circles they will be too dizy to fight. And they will be good company for each other

Cat and dog – 10

The 'self-interest' variation on the distraction theme. You allow each group to get so tied up with their own affairs and interests that they have no time to fight. The cat is too busy chasing the fish at the end of his tail, and the dog is too busy chasing the steak on the end of his tail. Since self-interest probably has a priority over fighting other people the system might well work.

Cat and dog – 11

The third-party concept. In this case the third party takes the form of the big super-power ally. The dog is chasing the cat and then a great big lion comes out and makes noises at the dog, and

then suddenly the dog decides that he might as well be friends with the little cat after all. Principle: if you have big friends you have fewer enemies.

Cat and dog – 12

A variation of the third-party concept. The cat and the dog are
fighting each other so the third party in the shape of a child or
baby comes along and pulls both their tails. They then stop
fighting each other and gang up on the child. This could also be
considered as a variation on the distraction concept.

The cat and dog fight each other.	A Child or Baby pulls There tales and then they join togther and	fight the child or Baby and so the are friends,

Cat and dog
Sighting

CHILD Child pulling cats tale.

dog and cat fighting child.

Cat and dog – 13

The cultural-assimilation concept. In other words, get used to your
enemy and then you may find that he is not so terrifying after all.
Put a toy dog in the cat's apartment, and a toy cat in the dog's
apartment. When they have finished barking at the toys and
chewing them about they suddenly realize that they are pretty
inoffensive and start learning to live with them. Then when the
cat and the dog meet in real life they will not have so much trouble.

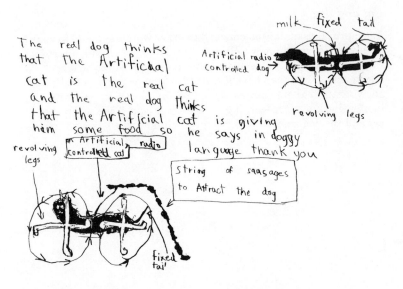

Cat and dog - 14

In this idea instead of there being toy cats and dogs there are
artificial radio-controlled cats and dogs which can walk about
using their circular legs which are painted on a revolving disc.
The real dog thinks that the artificial cat is the real cat, and the
real dog thinks that the artificial cat is giving him some food. So
he says in doggy language 'Thank you', and rather comes to like
the artificial cat. This liking is of course then transferred to a real
cat. You could only get an artificial radio-controlled cat to give
a dog some food.

Cat and dog – 15

A more sophisticated variation of the 'cultural-assimilation'
technique. Instead of having toy or radio-controlled cats and dogs,
you have the real thing. But you disguise the real thing. So the
cat is fitted out in a dog mask with false ears and also a false dog
tail for when it meets the dog. Similarly the dog is fitted out with
a cat mask and a false cat tail. So the cat looking from inside its
dog mask sees what appears to be another cat, and similarly the
dog looking from inside his cat mask sees what appears to be
another dog. So since the obvious cultural differences and points
of differentiation have been removed they can get on quite well
and discover the real personalities.

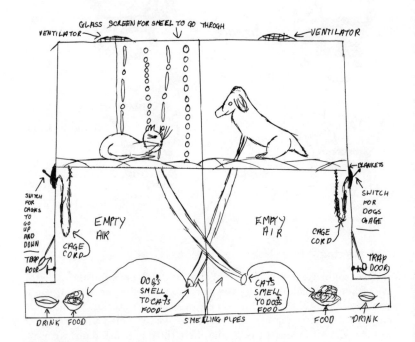

Cat and dog – 16

A more gradual process of cross-cultural assimilation. Cat and
dog live in separate apartments. But there is a tube from the cat
which comes out near the dog's food, and a tube from the dog
which comes out near the cat's food. This means that when the
cat goes to eat he gets the scent of the dog around his eating and so
learns to associate the dog's smell with good things. Similarly
when the dog is eating he can smell the cat and so learns to
associate the cat's smell with good food.

1 Smear your dog with cat food.

fishy meet

2 Smear your cat with dog food.

doggie licks

3

leave them alone as they scent each-others food

AND

friends

Cat and dog – 17

A further extension of the cultural-assimilation concept, but tying it in more directly to self-interest. The dog is smeared with cat food and the cat is smeared with dog food. When they meet each other they smell their own food, and so they get to licking each other and soon become friends. The principle is that business self-interest, if allowed free rein, may well overcome national or traditional animosities.

Mathew

Sophy

THE CAT
WITH ITS TONGUE
OUT
THE DOG DIVI-
ING IN

pond full of MILK

Cat and dog - 18

Instead of there being some
outside person who paints the
cat with dog food and the dog
with cat food, this is done
automatically by the individuals
concerned. There is a pond full
of milk and into it the dog
(wearing swimming trunks)
dives. On the bank stands the
cat with its tongue out waiting
to lick the dog clean as soon as
he comes out.

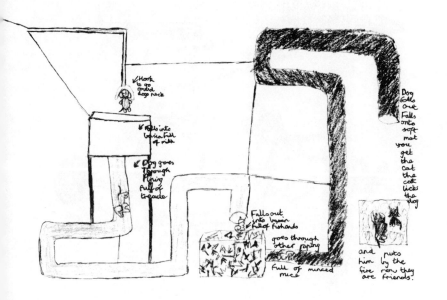

Cat and dog - 19

Nothing much is left to chance. A great deal of care is taken to make absolutely sure that the dog is acceptable to the cat. First of all he is dumped into a basin full of milk, and then he goes through a pipe which is smeared with treacle. He comes out of the treacle pipe and falls into a basin full of fish ends. From this he emerges to go through a tube full of minced mice. Finally, exhausted, he falls out of the tube to lie on a mat by the fire. The cat, unable to resist this mixture of goodies, immediately licks him all over and they become good friends. Possible principle: if you really think it worthwhile for people to become friends, and spare no effort to make it worthwhile, you may perhaps be successful.

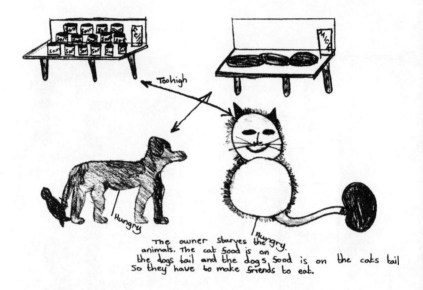

The owner starves the animals. The cat food is on the dogs tail and the dogs food is on the cats tail so they have to make friends to eat.

Cat and dog - 20

The mutual-aid concept. The cat is starved and so he is hungry. But the only way he can get his food is to eat it off the dog's tail. Similarly the only way the dog can get his steak is to eat it off the cat's tail; so they have to learn to get along with each other to get any meals. It might of course be argued that if the dog simply set off in pursuit of the cat he could get rather nearer to that steak.

BOTH ANIMALS HAVE TROUGHS FULL OF THE OTHER ANIMALS FAVOURITE FOOD. SO TO GET TO THEIR FAVOURITE FOOD, THEY HAVE TO BE FRIENDS TO SIDLE UP TO THE OTHER ANIMAL TO GET THEIR FAVOURITE FOOD.

Cat and dog – 21

Instead of simply tying the food to the tail of the cat or dog, this time there are special troughs, which are strapped alongside the bodies of the cat and dog. Since each trough contains the food of the other animal, they have to get alongside each other in order to eat. For some reason there is a bowl of cream attached to the cat's tail for when it goes on long journeys.

YOU PUT A CAT
IN ONE PART AND A DOG IN THE
OTHER WHEN THE CAT
STEPS ON A SMALL
BAR THE DOGS BONE
COMES DOWN AND
VICE VERSA . SO
WHEN THEY GO
NEAR EACH OTHER
THEY GET FOOD
SO THEY BECOME
FRIENDS

Cat and dog – 22

The whole mutual-aid thing here is formalized into a psychological
training cage, rather like a Skinner box. The only way they can
get fed is for one to feed the other by pressing on the bar. The cat
quickly learns that if he presses the bar the dog gets fed and looks
pleased. In return the dog learns that if he presses the bar the
cat gets fed and he looks pleased. So they now work very hard to
please each other, because they realize that it is only by pleasing
the other one that they end up by pleasing themselves. A view
that is perhaps cynical but immensely realistic.

The dog fishing for the cat with un under water gun

Butcher

Bones

The cat holding up the butcher for bones

Or give them love pills if the other method wont work

Cat and dog – 23

The mutual-aid thing is here carried to extremes. In the upper
part of the drawing the dog equipped with aqua-lung apparatus is
seen with a harpoon gun catching fish for the cat's supper. In
the bottom half the cat, with a sub-machine gun, is seen holding
up the butcher to obtain bones for the dog. If this method does
not work then you give them 'love pills'.

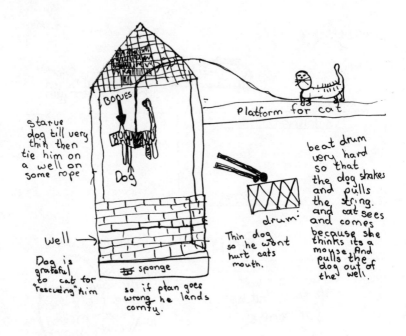

Platform for cat

starve dog till very thin then tie him on a well on some rope

BONES

Dog

well →

Dog is grateful to cat for "rescuing" him

sponge

so if plan goes wrong he lands comfy.

drum

Thin dog so he wont hurt cats mouth.

beat drum very hard so that the dog shakes and pulls the string. and cat sees and comes because she thinks its a mouse. And pulls the dog out of the well.

Cat and dog – 24

This could be called the 'inadvertent' mutual-aid concept. Or it could more simply be called the gratitude concept. What you do is beat the drum and this makes the dog jump about. The dog jumping about makes a string jump about, and so the cat thinks it is a mouse. The cat takes hold of the string and pulls it. This pulling on the string rescues the dog from the well. The dog is then immensely grateful to the cat and so from this gratitude springs a true friendship. Note that the designer has thoughtfully provided a sponge just in case the cat botches the rescue and the dog falls to the bottom. She also insists that the dog should be fairly thin otherwise the strain on the cat's mouth might be enough to hurt it.

I am holding the cat and the dog nose
to nose and strocing them

Cat and dog – 25

The direct-love concept. You hold the cat and dog nose to nose and
stroke them and so induce them to love each other. In fact the
preaching and practising of love.

Cat and dog - 26

If you don't trust your love-inducing power then you take the cat
and the dog along to a society which is a 'Friendly Society' and
therefore functions to make people friends. Unfortunately the
friendly society (like the United Nations) is a bit of a misnomer, and
does not serve to impart what it appears to promise.

Cat and dog – 27

Another variation on the direct-love concept. This time instead of
relying on human exhortation one relies on science. Both cat and
dog are put on the brain-washing machine. Note the packet of
washing powder at the base of the machine. Note also the bubbles
which come out whenever anything is washed. Cat and dog will be
brain washed into loving each other. Is that so awful?

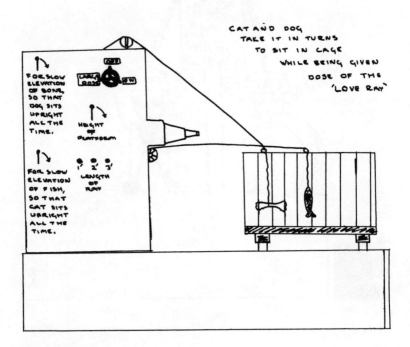

Cat and dog - 28

Another love machine. Cat and dog take it in turns to sit in a cage
and then they are made to sit upright when the bone (or fish) is
hoisted up. When they sit upright they are exposed to the full force
of the love machine, which induces in them this feeling of love –
presumably for everything in the world, since there is no actual dog
or cat in sight.

Variety

Perhaps the most striking thing about the attempts of the children to solve this political problem is the variety of approaches used. Each child decided in his own mind how he would tackle the problem, and then set out to tackle it in a definite way. Difference of approach is a very characteristic feature of children's thinking. If you put a group of adults in a room and ask them to tackle a problem they will have relatively few approaches distributed among them. But a group of children will come up with a much greater variety of approach. I have tried this out on a number of occasions and each time it is the same. It is probably not that children have a special ability to look at things in a different way, but simply that adults have almost completely lost this ability. So adults are always looking for the best and most sensible way and this only means the way which fits in best with their current ideas or experience. Since children have so little of this 'current' element in their experience or ideas, they are much freer to try out new ideas. Such ideas, though they may not seem very successful at first, can actually be carried further to give a useful and practical solution.

Direct

In tackling the cat-and-dog problem the children came immediately to the point. In each solution they show a simple and direct way of carrying out their idea of peace-making. There is no hesitation or messing around. If there is an effect to be achieved, then there is a simple and direct way of achieving it, and this the child shows.

Psychology

It might have been thought that the children would try and stop the cat and dog fighting simply by taking each one into a corner and giving it a good scolding, or else by shouting at them as they were fighting, and telling them 'to stop it at once'. It is after all the universal adult and political approach to stopping people from fighting. Indeed in the adult political world it is almost the only approach used. It is condemnation and exhortation. The psychology of children, however, seems to be a good deal better. They place little reliance on exhortation, or indeed on punishment. Instead they prefer to work through such things as the self-interest of the cat and the dog. Many of the designs were based precisely on this self-interest, and making it worthwhile for the cat and the dog to stop fighting simply because someone else has told them that it would be a good thing to stop fighting. They only expect the cat and the dog to stop fighting because the cat and the dog have realized that they can get what they want (e.g. food) much better if they stop fighting and cooperate.

The second psychological principle used by the children is that of distraction. If the cat and the dog are both fully occupied, and enjoying themselves, then they will have much less time for fighting. In other words the children realize full well that fighting is often the result of intense boredom, and that fighting provides the only interest and amusement in the lives of many people who are involved in such fights.

The third psychological principle used by the children is that of getting one side used to the other, and if necessary providing disguises or artificial aids for this purpose. Children are aware that it is often simple physical things like appearance and smell that become symbolic of the opponent you dislike (like skin colour). You can get the cat or the dog used to the other in a situation where he is not in any danger and is not terrified, and then gradually he will come to accept the difference and not be afraid of it. To my mind the thinking of children in tackling this problem shows a much better understanding of psychology than you find in politics either today or throughout the ages.

2 A Fun Machine

Design a fun machine.

Fun, pleasure, enjoyment are very abstract concepts which it is difficult to define. But fun is when you are having fun. It may be difficult to define, but fun is a very definite thing and you can recognize it at once. Fun is also very much part of a child's world. A child's world is fun centred. This is probably not the same as pleasure centred which is a much more adult thing. Given an opportunity to design a fun machine, would children choose a lot of 'fun' apparatus, or simply things which they enjoyed doing? Would the emphasis be on the hardware of fun or on the software (the mechanics of the situation or the mental response to a situation).

How greedy would children be? Would they want to have all the fun things they had ever known, or would they settle for one simple fun machine which they would use over and over again? What is fun for children? Is it a physical thing like jumping about? Or is it more like eating something you like? The basic problem is whether children would sit pondering the *definition* of fun, as most adults would, or whether they would regard it as a very real thing which can be brought about in a very real way, and then set out to design a machine that would have the effect of making it come about.

Fun – 1

A fun machine that goes along when you press a button. The
machine is a sort of store of all sorts of fun things like a box of
Lego, a box of bricks, a box of Meccano, a box of general toys and
a bookstall. (One of the compartments is simply the works of the
machine, to make it go when you press a button.) Here the
emphasis is on the fun machine being a collection of all sorts of fun
situations, and in this particular case mainly toys. Fun is having
something to play with.

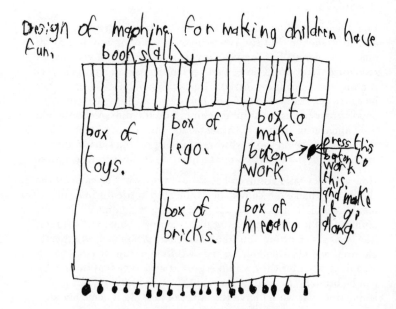

Fun – 2

A fun factory on wheels by a very
young designer. The factory does
all sorts of fun things like selling
you sweets and biscuits and
making toys. Why should the
factory be on wheels? Because
most fun things are on wheels, or
at least they 'do' something in
some way, and movement is the
simplest way of doing something.

horns that
hoot when button
pressed and
acaris pulling
factory
along

Fun factory on wheels.
Sells sweets and biscuits.
makes toys.

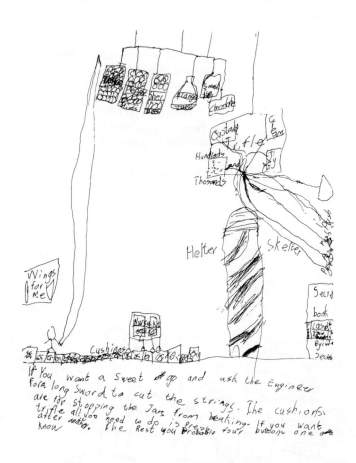

If you want a sweet go and ask the Engineer for a long sword to cut the strings. The cushions are for stopping the Jars from breaking. If you want trifle all you need to do is press four buttons one after another. The Rest you probably know.

Fun - 3

Another 'collection' type of fun machine. You put together all sorts of fun things and then you get what you want. Hanging from strings on a ceiling are all sorts of goodies like toffee, peppermints, sherbert, orange juice, Smash ice lollies and chocolate. 'If you want a sweet go and ask the engineer for a long sword to cut the strings. The cushions are for stopping the jars from breaking. If you want trifle, all you need to do is press four buttons, one after another. The rest you probably know.' In addition at the side there seems to be a set of wings, for the person to fly up and take the things down,

just in case the sword approach does not work. As everyone knows
trifle is made of cream, jelly, custard and hundreds and thousands
put together in a special way. So if you want a trifle you have just
got to press each of the buttons which releases one of these
ingredients, but unless you want them all mashed up together you
had better press the buttons in the right order. Since you are going
to be up in the air most of the time, you might as well have a
helter-skelter to enjoy coming down to ground again.

Fun – 4

A highly concentrated fun assembly. There is even a comment that
really there should be lots more things, but there is too little space
to put them in. There are luxury armchairs, a robot to obey your
commands, a switch panel which you press for any sort of food you
want, and a whole lot of books on the bookshelves (as an author
this is gratifying, because one knows that adults don't read books,
so it is nice to think that children still regard them as fun). It is not
quite clear how the Big Dipper or the football pitch come into the
picture, but since they are part of having fun it is as well to put
them in.

FUN MACHINE.

(P.S. LOTS MORE THINGS– TOO LITTLE SPACE)

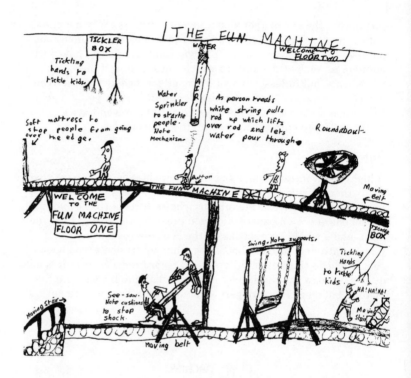

Fun – 5

Another assembly of fun things, but this time more in the sense of a
fun palace. On the ground floor there is a see-saw with careful
provision of cushions to stop you from getting that nasty judder
when you hit the ground. Also the swing and the tickler box which
provides tickling hands to tickle the kids and make them laugh.
Another tickler box is provided on the upper floor. An unusual
aspect of the fun to be had in this fun palace is the water sprinkler.
As you tread on the white string a rod goes up and lets water pour
through on top of your head - naturally this is a lot of fun.

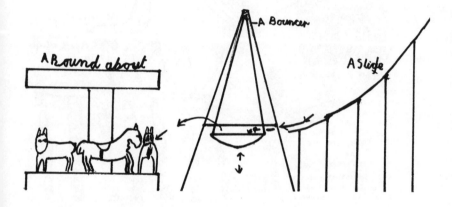

Fun – 6

The fairground approach to fun.
You go down a slide on to a
bouncer and then on to a
roundabout. Since it is a fun
machine all the parts must fit
together and it isn't a matter of
walking from one enjoyment to
another. They are all linked up in
some way. So all you have to do is
sit at the top of the slide and then
everything happens to you in
sequence.

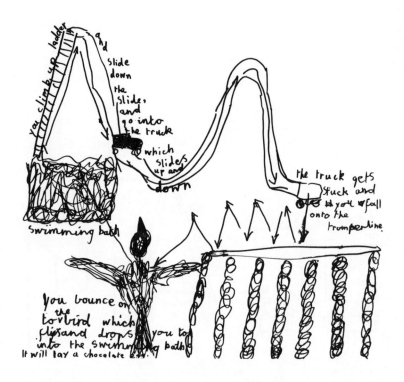

Fun - 7

Another sequence fun machine. You bounce on to the bird which
flies and drops you into the swimming pool (the bird will lay a
chocolate egg if you wish). Then from the swimming pool you climb
up a ladder and slide down into a truck which zooms up over a
hump and then comes down and stops rather suddenly, which
means that you fall off on to the trampoline with its great springs
and then back on to the bird again. So you go on going round and
round on this fun trip of sliding and bouncing and flying. You
probably eat the chocolate egg as you go along, or at least give it to
a friend. Bouncing and sliding and slipping seem very much to be
basic ingredients of fun.

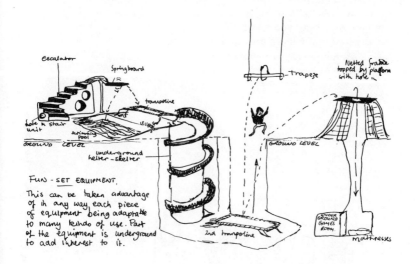

FUN - SET EQUIPMENT.

This can be taken advantage of in any way each piece of equipment being adaptable to many kinds of use. Part of the equipment is underground to add interest to it.

Fun – 8

More bouncing and sliding. Up an escalator on to a springboard, off that to a trampoline, then down a helter-skelter on to a second trampoline which shoots you up from on the ground on to a trapeze, and then on to a platform with a hole in it through which you fall down on to mattress underground. This time you have to find your own way back up to ground level and the start of the escalator.

Fun – 9

A very ordinary looking toy car,
with pedals which you turn to
make it go, but then there is a
unique feature. The unique
feature is the keyboard with lots
of buttons as shown in the
drawing. You press a button and
you get anything you want. For
instance if you want a tree house
then 'somehow' the tree house
appears.

a boy car with pedles for me to Drive
it. and with key boards of button I press for whatever I like such as a tree house.

Fun - 10

The ultimate simplification of press-button omnipotence. You simply
have a bracelet which you put on your wrist. Then when you want
something you just press the right button. This is perhaps the purest
form of the press-button idiom in any of the problem-solving efforts.
You press a button to get a television picture, and you press a
button to change that television picture, so why should you not be
able to press a button to get anything you want. All you have to do
is to buy the right machine, or for someone to make the right
machine. That is not your responsibility. All you have to do is to
know which button to press once you have got the machine. As I
have stated elsewhere, I think the growth of the press-button idiom
in thinking, is probably one of the most significant changes in
thinking for centuries. Its impact on adult thinking is much more
significant than is ever realized.

this is a thing wich you put
on your rist
and when you
want eny serten
thing you press
a diffrent button

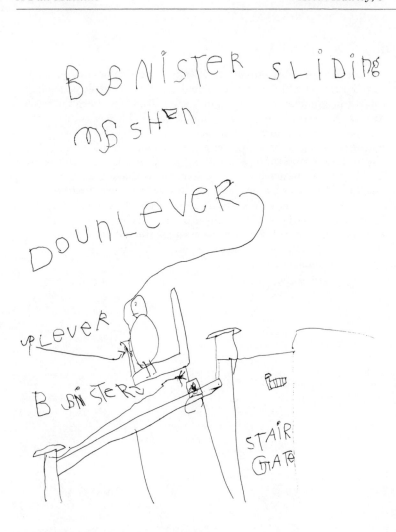

Fun - 11

In contrast to the previous designs, this designer has concentrated
entirely on one single aspect of having fun. Sliding down bannisters
is fun so if you have a machine to slide down bannisters, that is a
fun machine. The machine is operated by a lever.

Fun – 12

Tree-climbing is also fun so if you have a special machine to climb trees that will be a fun machine. The tree-climbing machine actually takes all the hard work out of tree-climbing, because it is operated by a battery. The machine operates by throwing a brass arm around the tree trunk and then proceeding upwards on its brass feet, rather like a lumberjack climbs a tree by throwing a loop of rope around it and then climbing up on his nail-studded boots.

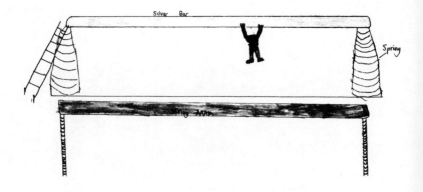

Fun - 13

Another single-minded design. This design comes back to the joy of
bouncing about. There is a silver bar (presumably chrome) which is
supported on springs, and this makes it very bouncy. So you bounce
from the bar to the spring mat and then up to the bar again and
down again, and go on bouncing for as long as you like.

Theres a dip in the mechanical horses neck
and theres a puzzle. The horse gallops along
and talks to me nicely It never wants
to stop. Unless i want it to
And it tries to buck me off.

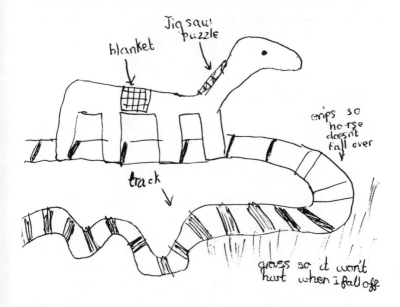

Fun - 14

Not quite so single-minded as the previous designs. This girl wants
to have her cake and eat it. Jigsaw puzzles are an indoor activity.
Horse riding is an outdoor activity. What you do is have a
mechanical horse with a jigsaw puzzle built into its neck. So as the
mechanical horse goes along its pre-set track you can get on with
the jigsaw puzzle. Because falling off a horse is not very pleasant
there are grips so that the horse does not fall over, and indeed if you
fall off there is grass so that you don't get too badly hurt. The
advantage of a mechanical horse is that it never wants to stop
unless you want it to stop, and also you could arrange it so that the
horse talked to you nicely.

Fun – 15

Cricket is fun too, only you have to go through all the bother of
having a lot of other people about, and if you are quite young it is
often difficult to get someone to bowl to you for hour after hour.
So a fun machine would be an automatic bowling machine which
bowls at you. And it works off a battery. A system of pistons and
weights catapult the cricket ball towards you and then you bat it
back and the whole thing starts over again.

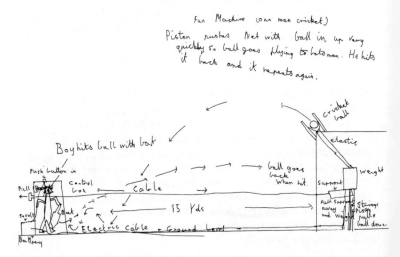

Fun Machine (one man cricket)

Piston pushes Net with ball in, up very
quickly so ball goes flying to batsman. He hits
it back and it repeats again.

Boy hits ball with bat

cricket ball

elastic

weight

ball goes back when hit

Push button in

Control Box

Cable

Support

Pull Support away and weight pulls ball down.

Strings pulls Piston ball down.

Pull

3 volt

Bat

15 Yds

Electric cable + Ground Level

Battery

Fun – 16

Most of the previous designs for fun have been rather vigorous
activities. This is really a water-music machine, with glasses and
bottles partly filled with water, and depending on how full they are
with water, they make a different note as you tap them. So by
having all these different glasses you can play music.

Name of this
Machine is
Water Music

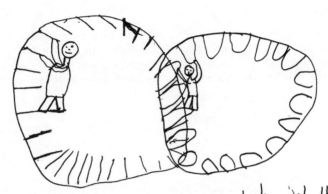

There are to circles one has planks and the other has archs. You must walk up the planks - or archs hold on and walk round and round. And as you walk round music comes out.

Fun - 17

Another music machine but this time combining the joys of music and some of the joys of physical activity.

Ready made

For their fun machines the children borrowed existing ready-made fun apparatus: some Lego, a box of Meccano, helter-skelter, trampoline, roundabout and so on. These were proven fun devices and their only defect was that they were not readily available the whole time. The child's only contribution to designing the fun machine was to think of the fun apparatus, or to assemble it with other fun apparatus in a particular way. Even when a new machine was designed, as for sliding down bannisters or climbing trees, this was to perform a fun activity which itself was very well known.

Collection

Most of the designers saw the problem as one of getting to, or having, fun machines. A natural way to solve this problem was to bring together all the fun machines that one could think of in one place, and this one place would be the fun machine. Many of the designs as a result were simply collections of fun ingredients brought together. The choice of fun ingredients varied from child to child. Some children might prefer playing with Lego or Meccano while other children might prefer watching television, or a football match or sliding down a helter-skelter. I doubt whether the choice is of any significance at all, but simply reflects what first came into the child's mind out of the multitude of opportunities for fun that he was aware of. Some of the designers worked hard to try and think of every conceivable source of fun and put them together. Other designers, however, took the easy way out and all they did was to assemble a collection of press buttons. This saved them the trouble of having to think of all the things that could be fun. Instead of actually providing the things you provided 'opportunity', which meant that as soon as you thought of something that could be fun you would simply have to press the right button and you would have it. But this is in fact quite an important design principle. Do you design for an actual situation, or do you design for flexibility and opportunity and a change of mind or use?

Satisfied

The fun-machine problem probably shows less actual originality or innovation than any of the other problems. This may be because children are themselves well satisfied with the fun machines that are available to them. The only snag is that these machines are not available often enough, and so they never really get a chance to get tired of them. If you have something that works very well why should you try and invent something new? In any case fun is such an abstract thing that you cannot invent a fun machine unless you know that it is going to be fun. The only way you can tell whether something is going to be fun is if it has already been fun in the past, or at least if that kind of activity has been fun in the past. It is not difficult to imagine an apparatus for building a house more quickly, but it is quite difficult to imagine a new apparatus which you believe would be fun. Fun is very much an experience, and in an experience you tend to go for what is tried rather than to generate something new about which you can tell very little. It may also be that, in tackling problems that are very familiar, the chances of coming up with a new approach or novel solution decrease the more familiar the problem is.

3 Weigh an Elephant

If you were the zoo keeper and wanted to find out how heavy an elephant was how would you do it?

Elephants are very large and very heavy. The purpose of this problem was to see how children dealt with this matter of size and weight. Would they treat the elephant like any other object to be weighed or would they take the great weight into special account? Magnitude is difficult to think about. You can distinguish very easily between a dog and a cat because they have different features but it is much more difficult to distinguish between a small box and a big box because they are both boxes.

But elephants are not boxes or lumps of concrete: they are living animals with personalities of their own. How would the children deal with this personality problem? Would they ignore it or make special provision for it? Would they treat the elephants as large inert weights or as large animals with feelings and wishes? Then there is the actual process of weighing. The idea of weight, balance and measurement is a difficult one but not uncommon in everyday life (kitchen scales, bathroom scales, etc.). Would children grasp the actual principles involved or just borrow complete machines for the purpose?

I would make a huge
Weigh ing mashine
and weigh the
elephant

Elephant - 1

A downright, no-nonsense solution to the problem. If you have
something very big to weigh then you simply make a HUGE
weighing machine. The sort of answer you might expect from the
chairman of a large company or a government minister, both of
whom would leave more exact solutions to their technicians.

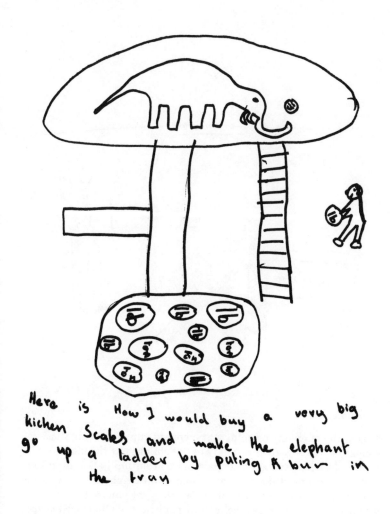

Here is How I would buy a very big
kichen Scales and make the elephant
go up a ladder by puting A bun in
the tray

Elephant - 2

Kitchen scales are for weighing things so for a very large thing you
need to buy very big kitchen scales. But the problem is not yet
solved because you have to get the elephant up into the scale pan.
This is done by providing a ladder for the elephant to climb and a
bun to tempt him to climb. A mixture of pound and ton weights will
tell you how much the elephant weighs.

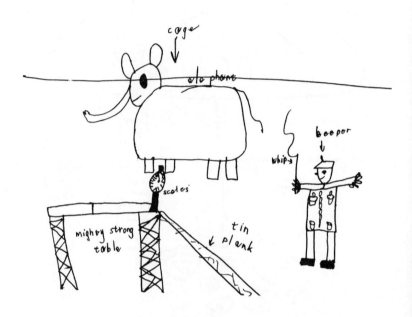

Elephant - 3

This problem of getting reluctant elephants up on to weighing-
machines was regarded by many of the children as the major
problem. These psychologists paid more attention to the intentions
and inclinations of the elephants than to the mechanics of weighing.
Reluctance to do something other people want you to do is not
unknown to children as a behaviour pattern. A well-dressed keeper
with a whip urges the elephant up the tin plank on to the mighty
strong table.

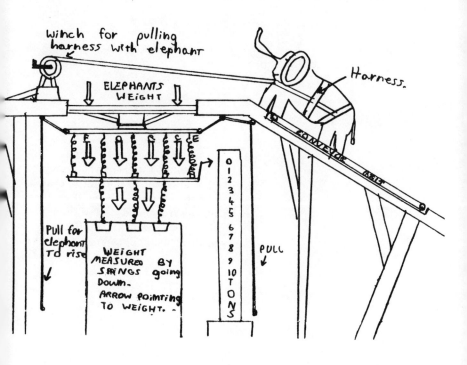

winch for pulling
harness with elephant

ELEPHANTS
WEIGHT

Harness.

CONVEYOR BELT

Pull for
elephant
To rise

WEIGHT
MEASURED BY
SPRINGS going
DOWN.
ARROW POINTING
TO WEIGHT. -

0
1
2
3
4
5
6
7
8
9
10
T
O
N
S

PULL

Elephant – 4

Another inclined ramp but this
time the elephant is winched up
as he stands on a free running
conveyor belt. The elephant steps
on to the weighing platform
which sinks down as the springs
are compressed. At the end you
have to pull a lever to bring the
elephant back up.

Elephant – 5

Instead of winching the whole
elephant up the ramp, you simply
haul up a bun on the bun railway
and the elephant follows after it
just as greyhounds follow the
the electric hare. The platform is
made of 'metal or steel'.

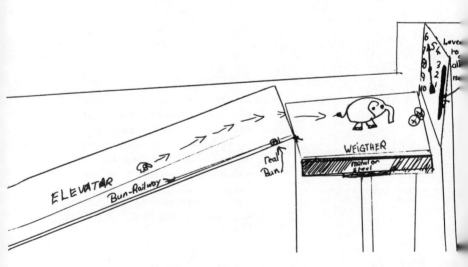

Elephant – 6

This problem-solver knows that even when you get an elephant up the ramp he can still hesitate at the edge of the weighing machine (like a reluctant horse being loaded into a horse-box). The elephant is tempted up a ladder by a bunch of bananas and then finds himself sliding willynilly down a chute and on to the weighing machine. The elephant may seem rather small in relation to the men but that is because if you draw the chute first the elephant has to fit inside it. In any case, he weighs two tons.

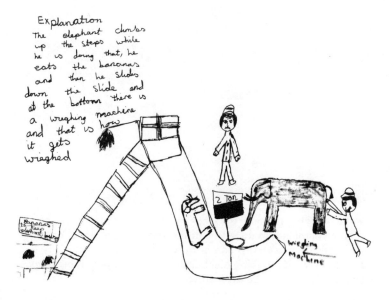

Explanation
The elephant climbs up the steps while he is doing that, he eats the bananas and then he slides down the slide and at the bottom there is a weighing machine and that is how it gets wieghed

Elephant - 7

Instead of trying to make the elephant walk on to the weighing
machine you pick him up with a crane and put him there. You need
a crane because elephants can be quite heavy. The
sideways/forwards looking elephant looks a bit like a flying duck.
There is a bun to soothe his feelings.

Elephant – 8

A single crane could overbalance so you had better have two – one on each side.

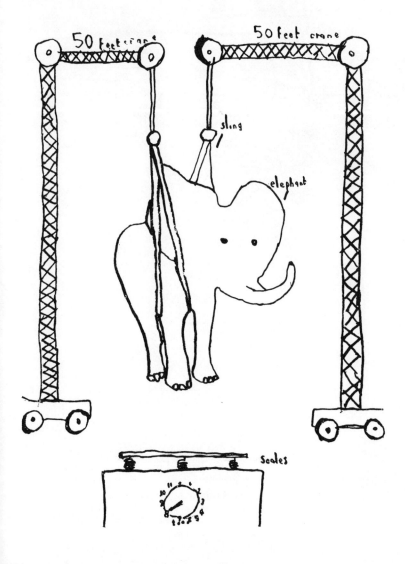

Elephant - 9

Cranes are used in industry to lift heavy weights but so are
fork-lift trucks. Not three elephants but the same elephant in three
stages of the process. As in previous drawings the weighing
machine works by the compression of springs.

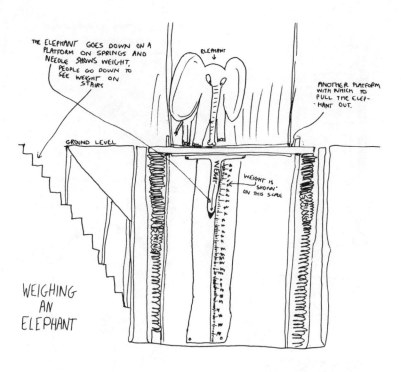

THE ELEPHANT GOES DOWN ON A
PLATFORM ON SPRINGS AND
NEEDLE SHOWS WEIGHT.
PEOPLE GO DOWN TO
SEE WEIGHT ON
STAIRS

ELEPHANT
↓

ANOTHER PLATFORM
WITH WHICH TO
PULL THE ELEP-
-HANT OUT.

GROUND LEVEL

WEIGHT

WEIGHT IS
SHOWN
ON THIS SCALE

WEIGHING
AN
ELEPHANT

Elephant – 10

The lateral-thinking solution. Instead of going to immense trouble
to get the elephant up on to the weighing machine you simply bury
the weighing machine in the ground and let the elephant stroll on
to it. At the end the platform is raised again to let the elephant get
off. The actual mechanism of the weighing machine is shown in
detail.

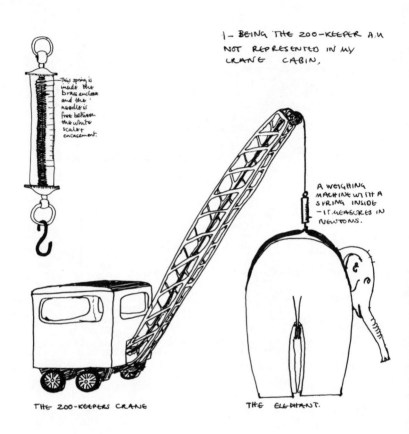

1 — BEING THE ZOO-KEEPER A.N NOT REPRESENTED IN MY CRANE CABIN.

This spring is inside the brass enclosure and the needle is free between the white scale encasement.

A WEIGHING MACHINE WITH A SPRING INSIDE — IT MEASURES IN NEWTONS.

THE ZOO-KEEPERS CRANE   THE ELEPHANT.

Elephant - 11

This time a crane is used not to put the elephant on to a weighing machine but to suspend the elephant from a spring-balance. Details of the spring-balance are given in the adjacent drawing. As the spring is stretched the pointer moves down the scale to give the weight of the elephant.

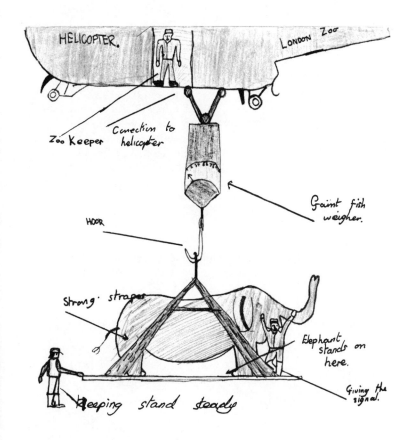

HELICOPTER.   LONDON ZOO

Zoo Keeper   Conection to
              helicopter

HOOK   Gaint fish
                                                     weigher.

Strong. straps   Elephant
                                                     stands on
                                                     here.

keeping stand steady   Giving the
                                                     signal.

Elephant – 12

Another spring-balance but not any old spring balance but a 'giant
fish weigher'. This makes sense because fish are certainly the
heaviest 'living' weight to be weighed. Instead of a crane to suspend
the balance there is a helicopter or 'sky-crane'. The elephant simply
moves on to the platform and the helicopter rises a little. Great
attention to organizational detail with one man giving the lift
signal and another steadying the platform which would otherwise
swing about.

Elephant – 13

A new design for a spring
weighing machine. The springs
are clock- (or clockwork-) type
springs and they can be wound up
with a handle. As you wind up
more and more springs the
tension increases until the weight
of the elephant is balanced. The
number of wound-up springs then
gives you the elephant's weight
in tons.

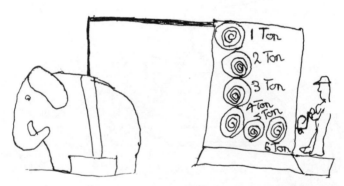

When the man turns
the handle round once it
it is one ton and twice
around two ton and so on
And When the elephant
gets o to the top of the
rope it tells you what the
a elephant weighs

Elephant – 14

Another new invention for a spring weighing machine this time
using the tension of a bending metal sheet. The elephant goes up
the stairs and walks across the sheet which bends under his weight.
You keep on lowering the plank of wood until the bending metal
sheet no longer rests on it. You can then read off the elephant's
weight from the level of the plank – as in a high-jump competition.
Although the plank is really just an indicator it has to be a 'very
thick plank of wood' since to begin with the elephant's weight
rests on it.

First the wood is put on the ½ ton shelf. Then the elephant
walks up the stairs. When he is on the metal it will bend under
his weight. If it touches the wood you know the elephant is more
than ½ ton. Then you take the elephant off and move the wood
on shelf down. Give the elephant something nice to eat, then
make him go onto the metal again. When the metal does not touch
the wood you know he is however many tons the last
shelf was.

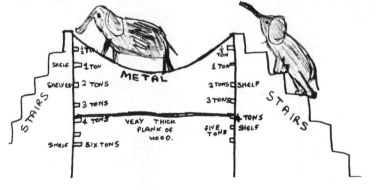

Elephant – 15

A change from springs to a well
thought out hydraulic weighing
system. Water is pumped from a
tank into a cylinder to raise the
ramp supporting the elephant
platform (like a hydraulic lift in a
garage). The pressure which
supports the ramp is indicated by
the gauge and this gives the
elephant's weight. The rear view
of an elephant is rather easier to
draw than the front view.

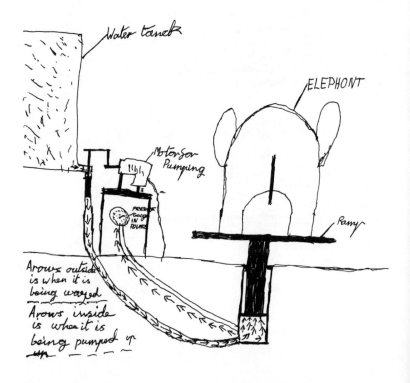

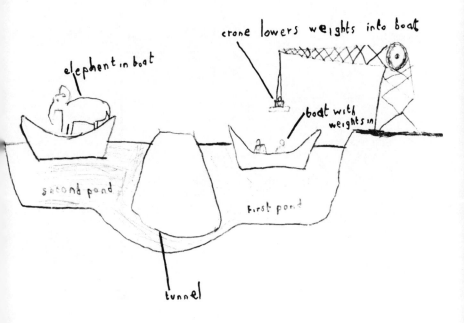

crane lowers weights into boat

elephant in boat

boat with
weights in

second pond

first pond

tunnel

Elephant – 16

Another water-filled system. It seems to be based on the
conventional scales with the two pans connected by water instead
of a beam. Readers can try and figure out whether the system would
actually be usable or not. The answer is not easy.

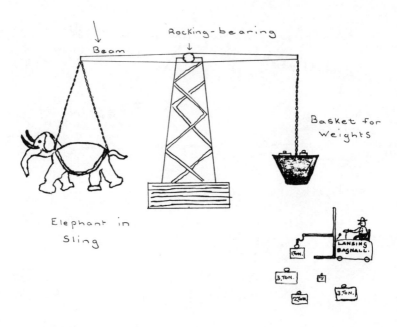

Elephant in Sling

Elephant - 17

The conventional beam scale. A fork-lift truck is used to get the heavy weights up on to the pan. The available weights range from one to three tons and give some idea of the expected weight of the elephant.

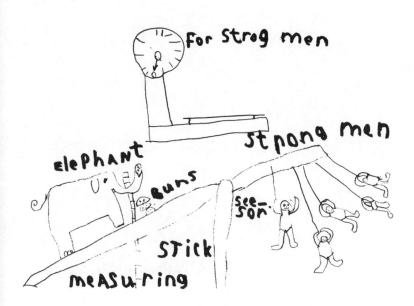

Elephant – 18

A two-stage process. Tempted by buns the elephant walks up the
ramp. Then several 'strong men' who have already weighed
themselves on the human scales swing from the beam. More men
join the swingers until the elephant takes off. A measuring stick
tells when this is happening.

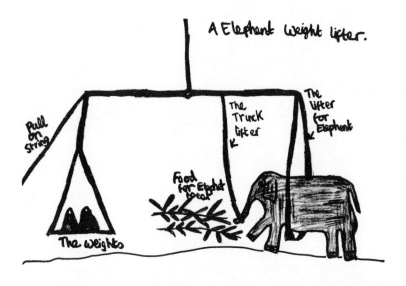

Elephant – 19

A special 'trunk lifter' to prevent the elephant from cheating by holding on to the food or the ground and so giving a false weight.

Elephant – 20

This elephant weighs himself by making use of the unique
advantage offered by his trunk. Judging from the weights he is
using he seems to be indulging in some wishful thinking.

Elephant – 21

A very simple and very clever solution. The elephant is too big for ordinary household scales. So you get four such scales and make him stand with one leg on each – then you add up the four weights (about half a ton could be weighed in this way). I have used the method myself with people too heavy to be weighed on ordinary scales. The elephants tusks seem to curve the wrong way.

plug pops out to show weight

air pump

rubber air belt

Elephant – 22

A figure-conscious young lady who has got girth and weight mixed
up. The corset is pumped up and then a plug pops out so indicating
the pressure in the corset. For a given air input this pressure will
be related to the girth. It may well be that as with humans fat
elephants are heavy elephants.

Elephant – 23

Someone has ducked the main problem by choosing to weigh a baby elephant. Or it may be easier to identify with a baby one.

Magnitude

On the whole the children appreciated that elephants were big and heavy. This could be seen by the specification of steel or 'mighty strong' platforms, by the use of ton weights, and by the need for such devices as cranes and fork-lift trucks.

Psychology

A lot of the children seemed more concerned with the psychology of the elephant and the difficulty of getting him on to the weighing machine than with the actual weighing which was taken for granted. Buns, bananas and branches were offered as temptation.

Mechanism

A few children simply borrowed available weighing devices such as a fish-weigher or kitchen scales but most of them actually designed special weighing machines using springs or water pressure, etc. Such designs showed an extremely good grasp of the principles involved.

Function

When children want to achieve a certain function they are very good at borrowing machines which give that function even if it is not the main function of the machine. Helicopters, fork-lift trucks and clock springs are examples of this sort of function borrowing. This ability to actually separate out the function from the total idea of a machine is strong in children and surprises many adults.

4 Build a House Quickly

If you wanted to build houses more quickly, how would you do it?

The problem is to do something that is already done, but to do it 'more quickly' – to speed things up, to achieve some sort of new efficiency. The speeding-up process might be a speeding up of the whole building process, or it might be a speeding up of some part of it. Another way would be to take some part of the process and change it, or maybe even drop out some part of the process. Or would the children decide that instead of speeding up the existing process they would like to change it and invent a new process or invent a new way of building houses completely?

Speed is a fairly abstract concept. You can tell whether a car is going faster than another car, but how do you tell that you are building a house quickly? Is it simply the rate at which you put the bricks down, or the convenience with which you put the bricks down? Is it the number of stages you have to go through, or is it simply a matter of speeding up the transport of different bits and pieces to the place where you need them?

Achieving speed and efficiency in processes are very real problems, both in business organization and in organizations in general. In particular the building of houses more quickly is a real problem to virtually every government.

House - 1

A direct conceptual solution. If you had a wizard and he could do magic, and he said 'Abracadabra!' then you could build a house very quickly. This is not as mad and impractical as it may seem. In Chicago recently, where a building schedule was as much as two years behind time, the constructor hired a 'wizard' foreman and within a few months the construction was ahead of schedule. (In fairness it should perhaps be mentioned that the Mafia is suspected of having had something to do with the affair.) On the whole this sort of problem-solving is too much neglected in business and government.

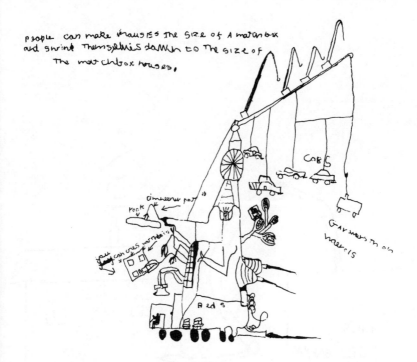

people can make hauses The size of A matchbox
and shrink Themselves dahh to The size of
The matchbox houses,

House - 2

This time you make the houses the size of matchboxes, and then
the people shrink themselves down to fit the size of matchbox
houses. The machine shown deals with matchbox houses and
matchbox cars, and does everything that needs doing to them. The
general concept from this is that you do whatever can be done
quickly and simply and then you adapt yourself to the result. In
practical terms perhaps not a bad principle.

House - 3

The houses are baked intact in a big kiln, and then a mechanical
arm takes them out and puts them on their site complete, down to
smoke issuing from the chimney. The idea is that the house is built
as a single unit, just as a jar or other piece of pottery is put
together, placed in the oven and comes out complete. Unlike all the
other designers, this designer has chosen to make houses as a
complete unit, rather than build them up from bits and pieces.

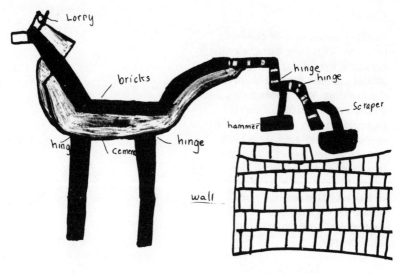

Aim. is to have a mechanical
bricklayer and so speed
up the building work
The cement and bricks are pre-
mixed and they move along a belt
to the site.

House – 4

One part of the house-building process is speeded up. The most
time-consuming job is laying the bricks, so to speed up house
building you have a mechanical bricklayer. In this bricklayer the
cement and bricks are pre-mixed and then they move along a belt
and get put on the wall. In addition there is an automatic scraper,
which prepares the bed on to which the bricks are going to be laid.
So the bricks move directly from the lorry to the site where they are
to be placed without any human intervention. There is no
indication as to how the machine decides where to place the brick.

House – 5

Another automatic brick-laying
machine. This time using waving
antennæ for taking the bricks
off the pile and putting them on
the building. A separate tube
pours out a quantity of cement
just underneath where the brick
is going to be placed. This time
the bricks are placed according
to a large control board. The
control board can also be seen
to have a little oscilloscope
window with the usual sort of
patterns you see on an
oscilloscope.

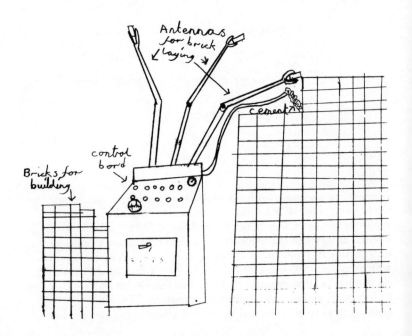

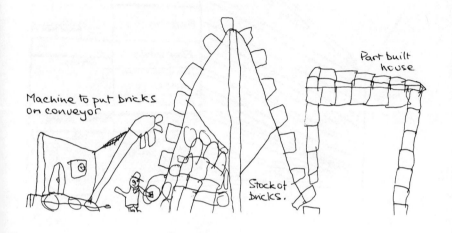

Machine to put bricks on conveyor

Part built house

Stock of bricks.

House – 6

There is a crane-like machine to put bricks on a conveyor belt.
The bricks are then hauled right up into the air, and then come
down again on the other side to start building the house. It seems
that the designer thought that the conveyor-belt idea would be
good, and then got rather carried away by the idea, so that the
conveyor belt becomes almost an end in itself. It seems to introduce
a rather unnecessary journey on the part of the bricks. One must,
however, bear in mind that the height of the conveyor belt is to
allow you to build rather high houses, even though the conveyor
belt at the moment is shown laying bricks at a rather low level.
Presumably the down slope on the conveyor belt can be raised to
whatever is the height of the house. In my experience I don't ever
recall having seen a conveyor belt giving bricks to the man who is
laying them. This would seem quite a simple idea which could be
put into practice immediately – if it does not already exist.

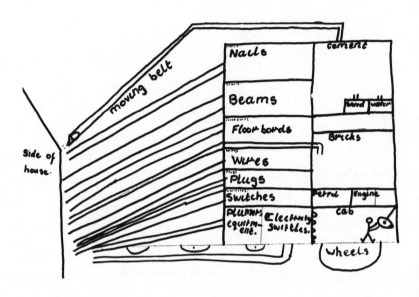

House - 7

The conveyor-belt idea multiplied up to deal with all the ingredients of a house – such as nails, beams, floor-boards, wires, plugs, switches, plumbers' equipment and so on. Each one of these is stocked on its own shelf and can move to the house along a pre-set channel. The designer has clearly focused on transport as that part of the building process which slows things down. If you can get the necessary materials you need to the place you need them quickly, then the house-building process would be speeded up very much. It is certainly true in major construction works that one of the most important problems is to get the vast amount of material needed to the site when it is needed. Delays in this are certainly a major factor in building speed.

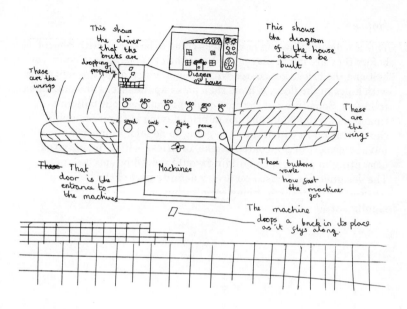

This shows the driver that the bricks are dropping properly

These are the wings

This shows the diagram of the house about to be built

Diagram of house

100 200 300 400 500 600

speed limit flying pressure

These are the wings

These That door is the entrance to the machines

Machines

These buttons varie how fast the machine go's

The machine drops a brick in its place as it flys along.

House - 8

Brick transport this time is by a flying brick-layer. The machine
flies over the site and carefully drops bricks where they are
required. The driver is provided with a diagram of the house that
is to be built, and also with a little television monitor screen to
show him that the bricks are dropping where he intends to drop
them. There is a row of buttons which tell you how fast the
machine is going, and also a row of indicators to tell you the speed,
the pressure and so on. On this occasion the designer is not only
concerned with how to get the bricks quickly to where they should
be placed, but also with strict control of how they are being placed.

House – 9

This is a design showing how bricks come to be coated with cement
before they are put in place. The box of bricks goes along a conveyor
belt and the bricks get coated with cement which drips through a box
with holes in the floor. A hand then picks up the bricks and puts them
in layers. Something of the sort could presumably cut building
time because much of the time in brick-laying is spent on laying
the mortar on to which they are going to be laid. If one were to
have some sort of pre-coated bricks, or bricks which did not need
cementing in place, then building would indeed be speeded up.
The designer has focused on a very definite part of the building
process, which though it may seem rather small is certainly very
significant.

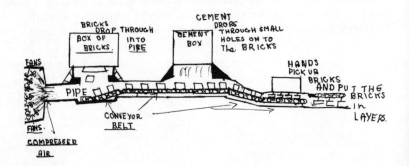

House - 10

Further attention to this problem of getting cement on to the
bricks when they are put in place. The cement is poured out of
a large jug by a mechanical arm. Another mechanical arm is
laying the bricks. You pour the cement into a hopper and then it
travels up a pipe and comes out in a tube just over the jug, so
that whenever the jug is empty it can be refilled immediately.
An interesting point is that in order to get the cement travelling
up the tube cement magnets are provided. These magnets act
through the walls of the tube and attract the cement upwards.
In order to keep the cement properly mixed there is a mixer which
puts an arm into the pipe and stirs the cement around.

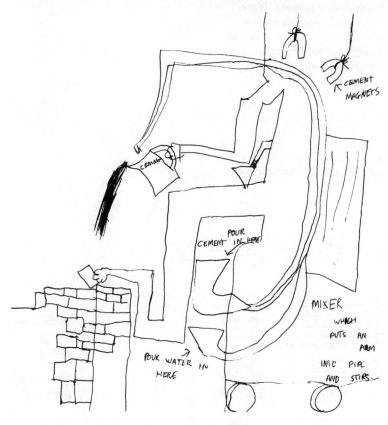

House – 11

New materials. A crane with a
special lifting mechanism lifts
glass-fibre panels into position.
Once they are in position then
the outside of this rather flimsy
glass-fibre house is sprayed with
cement which sets hard and
gives you a solid house. The
speeding-up process here comes
about because there is complete
elimination of the slow brick-by-
brick-laying process. Were
house building not such a
traditional industry, it seems
likely that something of the sort
would be in effect already.

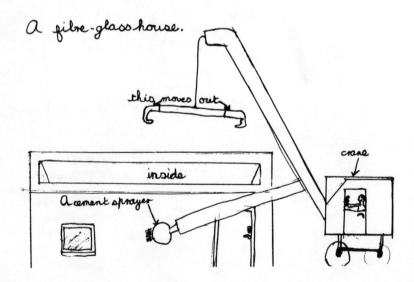

a fibre-glass house.

this moves out

inside

crane

a cement sprayer

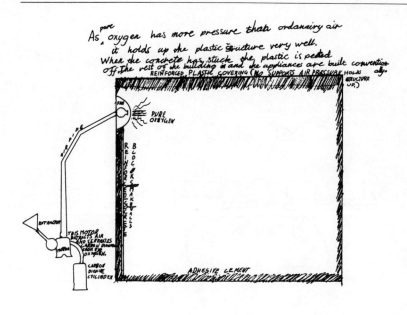

House - 12

Another coating system. Pure oxygen which 'has more pressure
than ordinary air' holds up the plastic structure very well.
Adhesive cement is then sprayed on to the walls, and when the
concrete has set the plastic is peeled off. The basic idea is similar
to the previous design, except that this time an inflatable
structure is used as the base to which the concrete is attached
instead of a constructed glass-fibre structure. This would, in fact,
make house building even quicker. On a lesser level inflatable
shuttering for conventional concrete work would seem to be a
good idea.

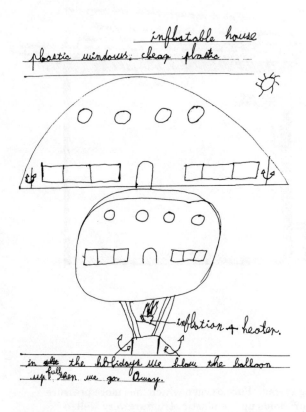

House – 13

Direct inflatable house which is blown up full in the holidays
and then allowed to collapse when 'we go away'. Inflation is
achieved by means of hot air coming from a little heater, and the
house is inflated just as a hot-air baloon is inflated. The bottom
half of the drawing shows the house being inflated by this hot air,
and the top half shows the house as it is completely inflated. Note
the change in shape, in the size of the windows and the doors of
the house, as it gets inflated. Initially they are small and they
become bigger as the whole house expands in size.

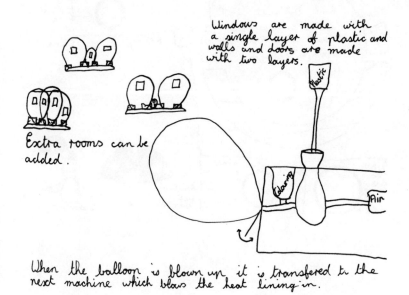

Windows are made with a single layer of plastic and walls and doors are made with two layers.

Extra rooms can be added.

When the balloon is blown up it is transfered to the next machine which blows the heat lining in.

House - 14

More inflatable houses, though this time on a rather more
permanent basis. Neutral plastic is poured into a container, and
then it is blown along by air, colour is added and finally the plastic
is blown into a balloon. When the balloon is blown up it is
transferred to another machine which then blows the 'heat'
insulation lining into the first balloon. The balloon sets solid.
Houses are then an assembly of these balloon-like structures. If
you want a bigger house, or more rooms, you simply add another
balloon. This is an immensely attractive idea. One might imagine
large plastic balloons being put together and then going inside to
cut out the pieces that are redundant in order to give you as much
space as you like inside.

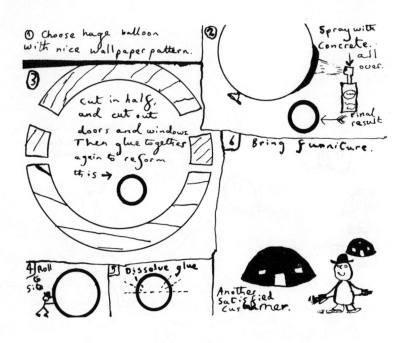

① Choose huge balloon with nice wallpaper pattern.

② Spray with concrete. all over.

← Final result

③ cut in half, and cut out doors and windows. Then glue together again to reform this is →

⑥ Bring furniture.

④ Roll to side

⑤ Dissolve glue

Another Satisfied customer.

House - 15

You choose a huge balloon with a nice wallpaper pattern and blow it up, and then you spray it with concrete all over. This gives you a solid sphere which you cut about a bit, and then reassemble.

House – 16

A direct and very simple idea. You have a square coil of rope which you lay in an igloo fashion putting glue between each layer and when this has set you have a solid house. One might imagine this system actually working with concrete impregnated rope which is coiled round and round to give a structure. When the structure is complete you 'cut out' doors and windows.

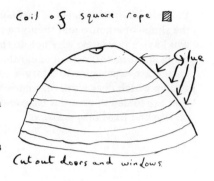

Coil of square rope

Glue

Cut out doors and windows

Concertina or Chinese lantern

pull up

House – 17

A concertina-type house, which is very easy to pack and transport and when you get to where you want you open out the concertina and provide some central support. In a sense like a tent but much more permanent. After all, one only wants walls for weather protection, and the weight-supporting part of the house can be quite different. The beauty of the concertina house is that there is no assembly work at all to be done on the site, not even the fixing of panels to a basic structure.

House - 18

You can buy little sheets of cardboard from which you cut out
the shape of a house and then you fold the flaps as indicated and
you have a house. So why not do this on a large human scale by
using sheet metal instead of cardboard? A direct transfer from
immediate experience to a larger scale. This is in fact a building
system which does work on somewhat similar lines, with walls
that are folded in on a flat base and then the walls are folded out
on site and fixed into position.

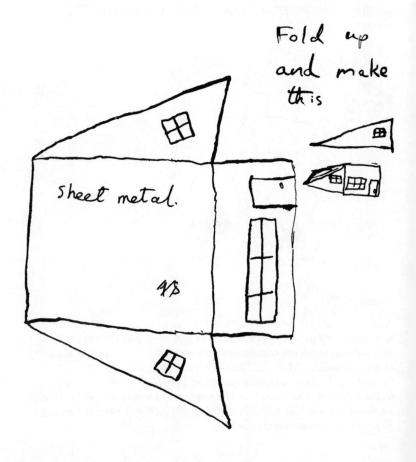

House – 19

Away from traditional materials like bricks and cement to a
plastic house. Outside plastic walls are moulded at the factory,
and then inside plastic screens are used to divide the house into
bathroom, bedroom, dining room and kitchen. The advantage of the
circular structure is that the walls can be moulded in one piece,
or at least in identical panels which can be fitted together. In this
design there is no attempt to try and speed up the existing
technology, but simply to provide a new technology.

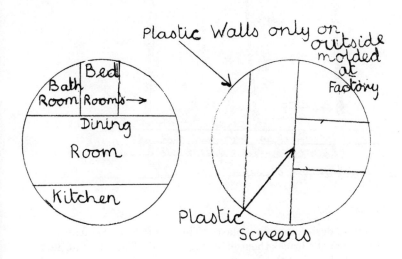

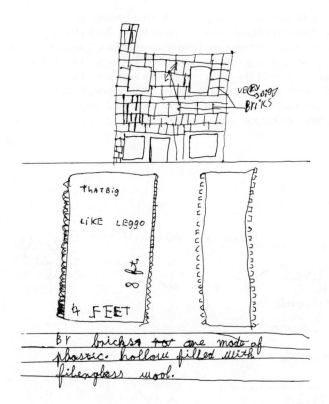

House - 20

Another design that uses plastic. This has two central features.
First that the bricks themselves are very big. They are four feet
by eight feet. But they are not very heavy because they are made of
plastic, and they are hollow and filled with fibre-glass wool, which
acts as insulation. The advantage of having very big bricks is
clearly that you can build a house very quickly with them. The
big bricks are rather like Lego bricks which mean that they have
knobs on them, and you can fit them together simply by pressing
them together. This gets rid of the bother of having to put in
cement and so on. Another example of 'transfer' or 'scaling up'
in problem-solving.

House - 21

The house is built of ready-made panels which are fitted together
in rather a special way. Each panel is edged with strong magnetic
metal, and so all you have to do to fit them together is simply to
put them in position, and then the magnets will hold them together
for ever. This is certainly very much quicker than having to screw
the panels together or nail them together in some way. It might be
argued that the magnetic metal would be very expensive or would
soon wear out, and yet one could go on from this idea to some
sort of temporary magnetic band which one would use to hold the
pieces together while some longer acting material like glue or
cement was allowed to set. Even this would speed up the
attachment process considerably. Note the use of magnetic adhesion
as a type of instant adhesion which can be stored permanently and
which comes into effect immediately - there are not many other
adhesives which have these qualities.

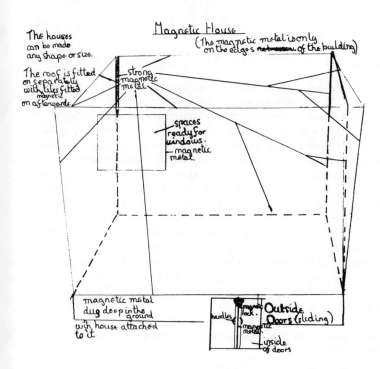

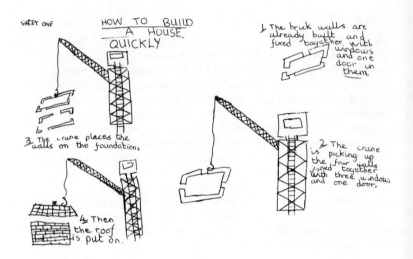

House - 22

Follow the sequence of construction. Basically the construction
consists of prebuilt units which are placed in position by a
gigantic crane. The walls are fitted together and then picked up
by the crane and put on the foundations. Then the roof is put on.
Note that the next operation is to take the roof off again and put
in the whole of the downstairs at once. This is followed by putting
in the downstairs ceiling leaving a space for the stairs. After this
the upstairs is put in, then the actual roof is put on again. Note
the significance of putting the roof on and then taking it off again.
This is exactly the sort of operation that at the moment does slow
down building so very much. You do something and then you have
to undo it in order to do something else. This is seen very clearly
in road building, where you build a road and only after you build
it do people come along and dig it up and put down drains and
cables. In fairness to the designer, when the roof is finally put on
it is referred to as 'the actual roof'. This may suggest that the first
roof to be put on was only a temporary roof so that people could
work underneath it and get on with finishing the interior of
the building.

SHEET TWO

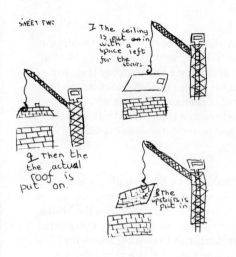

7 The ceiling is put on in with a space left for the stairs.

9 Then the the actual roof is put on.

8 The upstairs is put in

5 Then the roof is taken off again.

6 The whole of the downstairs and some stairs is put in at once by a crane.

Improve

The designers looked at the existing process of house building and
decided that they were going to improve it in some way. Most of
them chose to improve it by providing a more speedy transport of
materials to the place where they were needed. Another method
of improvement was to get rid of human labourers who might
slack, be lazy or just tire, and replace them with an automatic
machine which never tired and never needed tea-breaks.

Focus

Several designers chose to speed up the house-building process by
focusing directly on one single aspect of that process and
improving this aspect. For instance, if you pre-coated the bricks
with cement then this would speed up the process by eliminating
the need for using cement or mortar at the actual moment of
brick-laying. In improving any process this is a very effective
principle: look at a part of the process which provides the major
source of inefficiency, and then tackle just this single aspect of
the process, instead of trying generally to tart up things all round.

Change

There were those who were not content to improve the existing
process but preferred to introduce completely new technology.
Outstanding among this group were those who suggested spraying
concrete on to basic structures or blowing up houses, which could
either be left as inflated houses or then coated with concrete.
Another type of innovation was not so much in the way in which
concrete was used, but in using new materials, for instance plastic.
Surrounded by plastic and concious of the way it can easily be
moulded in a factory, many children wonder why plastic is not
more often used in house building.

Effective

It is quite easy to change a process or to provide a new process
instead of existing ones. It would have been easy for the children to
come along with some other way of building houses. But in fact
every single one of the designers kept carefully in mind the
specification of the problem – that the new way of building the
house should be quicker than the old way. Every one of the

suggestions at first sight seems to provide a change for the
quicker. There is no design which is change for the sake of change.
The ability to keep the problem specification in mind is impressive.

Invent a Sleep Machine

Design a special bed for people who have difficulty in going to sleep.

Very few children have difficulty in going to sleep. The problem is essentially an adult problem. How would the children tackle it? Would they produce their own ideas on what makes a person go to sleep, or would they simply borrow sleep-making devices from the adult world which they had experienced perhaps in their parents or read about? Would the emphasis be on things that made a person go to sleep, or on removing those things that kept the person awake? The problem itself is not a mechanical problem like some of the other problems but the production of a very definite state. Would the children use mechanical means to bring about this state, or would they use psychological means, or a combination of both.

The big difference between this and the other problems is that in the other problems there was always a man 'doing something', arranging something, controlling something. But in this case it is the man himself who is the object. Something is happening to the man. How then is this going to be brought about, if it is the man who is going to do something to the man, and once it is done, the man is no longer able to control anything – because he is asleep.

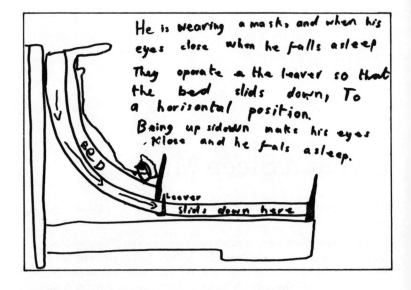

Sleep - 1

Perhaps suggested by those dolls which close their eyes when you
tip them up. The idea is that if you tip up the bed then the man's
eyes close and he goes to sleep. When he is asleep however there
is not much point in leaving him standing on his head. So one needs
some sort of mechanism to turn off the sleep-inducing machine
once the man is asleep. This is achieved by having a mask and
through this mask the closing eyes operate a lever, which can be
seen in the drawing. Once this lever retracts then the bed slides
down under its own weight and assumes the horizontal position.
Note the practicality of the design, for instance in the large
headboard which prevents the man sliding off the bed when his
feet are near the ceiling. Note also the board at the end which
prevents the bed itself from sliding off the support when it slips
down into the horizontal position.

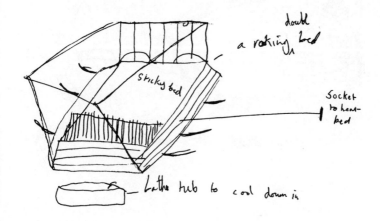

doubl
a rocking bed

sticky bed

Socket
to heat
bed

Lathe tub to cool down in

Sleep - 2

The movement this time is more
conventional, being an ordinary
rocking movement. The ends of
the rockers can be seen projecting
from the sides of the bed. Since
it is a rocking bed you might
well slide off, so the bed is a
special sticky bed. An electric
wire goes to a socket to provide
heat for the bed, but at the same
time there is a tub to cool down
in, so you can get your
temperature just right.

Bed to make you go to sleep.
Cats tied to rockers

Cats try to catch rubber mice attached to spring.

cats harness

Spring pulls mice back and forth wich makes cats pull rockers.

Sleep - 3

Another rocking bed, though this time the rocking is fore and aft.
Rocking however is not left either to chance or to your own
movements. Instead a very carefully designed animal-power rocking
mechanism is provided. Two cats are attached to the rockers, and
as they chase after mice which pop in and out of a hole, they rock
the bed. The mice are special rubber mice attached to a spring, as
shown in the drawing. This spring makes them go back and
forwards so bobbing in and out of the hole. Since it is very unlikely
that the cats would exactly synchronize their movements, or for
that matter that the mice would, the resulting motion would most
certainly provide a rocking movement for the bed. Presumably the
person goes to sleep and after a time the cats also get tired and
go to sleep.

Sleep - 4

Up and down movement with large bouncy springs. Energy is
provided by some sort of motor which you wind up with the handle
provided. This gives you a limited amount of movement and when
that movement runs out you are either asleep or you have to jump
out of bed and wind it up again. Really rather a practical device.
There seems no reason why such a device should not be in actual
production, even if only in the form of a rocking cradle for children.

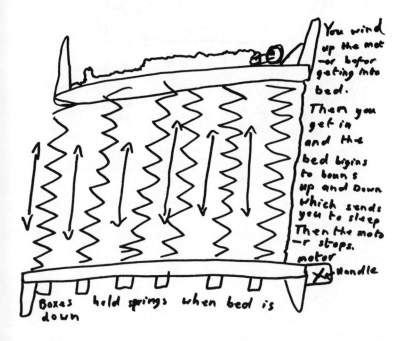

Sleep – 5

Here the movement part consists only of a springy mattress, but there are several other things in addition to movement to make the person go to sleep. For instance there is the 'Boots' hot-water bottle filled with hot perfume to soothe the person. There is also an automatic lullaby coming from a radio, which is switched on as soon as the person's head touches the pillow. Thoughtful provision of blankets as well, since being cold can certainly keep a person awake.

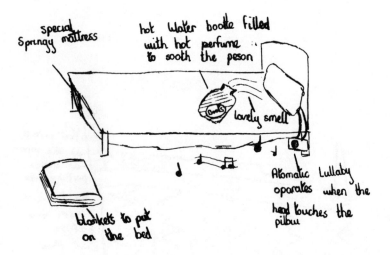

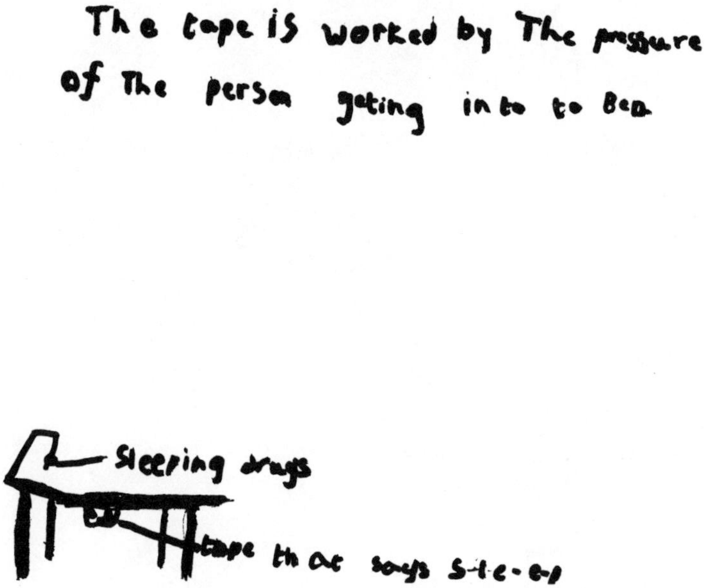

The tape is worked by The pressure
of The person geting in to to Bed

Sleeping drugs

tape that says S-l-e-ep

Sleep – 6

Another example of automatic operation. This time the weight of
the person getting into bed operates a tape recorder that says
'S-l-e-e-p, sleep, sleep'. It is not quite clear how the tape recorder
gets switched off, when the person has actually gone to sleep, or
perhaps it just goes on and on as a sort of loop in case he wakes
up during the night. If the tape recorder is not sufficient some
sleeping drugs are suspended quite conveniently over the person's
head.

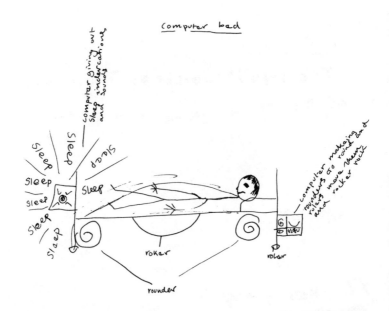

Computer bed

computer giving out
sleep indercations
and sounds

Sleep
Sleep
Sleep
Sleep
sleep
Sleep
Sleep
sleep

computer makaing
roundexs go round and
rolexs move sleep and
roker rock

roker

rounder

roker

Sleep - 7

This is another automatic design, with a tape recorder calling out
'Sleep - sleep - sleep' in a hypnotic manner. This time the process
is controlled by a computer. But in addition to this tape recorder
there is also a rocking movement. This rocking movement is
provided in an extremely ingenious manner. There are spiral
springs as shown, and as these spiral springs go round and round
they very gently lift the bed up and down. This is a highly original
and inventive design for a rocking mechanism, since the mechanism
will be very smooth and undulating because of the nature of the
springs. In effect the child is using springs as a sort of cam
mechanism, but it is very much better than a cam mechanism
because the action is so much smoother.

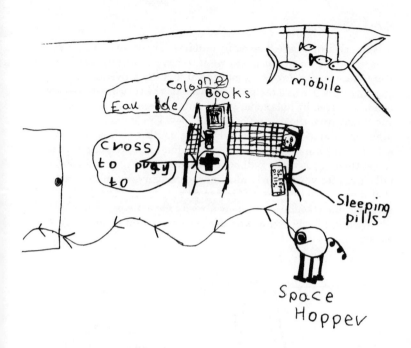

Sleep - 8

A 'total' type design – that is to say a design where everything that
can be thought of is put in. There is a cross to pray to, eau de
cologne, books to read, a mobile to look at, and sleeping pills in
case everything else fails. In addition there is a space hopper,
which can be looked at as it hops out of the door. The emphasis
seems to be on comfort and having everything you want around
you and then you go to sleep, a bit like the burial of the Pharoahs
in ancient Egypt.

Sleep – 9

It is interesting to see how many children do not rely on a single
sleep-inducing mechanism, but want to have additional mechanisms.
Here there is also a rocking movement and the provision of
sleeping pills. Unlike the previous designs the rocking movement
is not achieved by balancing the bed on rockers, but by having it
suspended from the ceiling by thick ropes. This gives rather a
different kind of rocking – a much more gentle one from side to
side. If you want the sleeping pills you don't have to get out of bed
to get them, you simply pull on a rope, and this releases a sleeping
pill right into your mouth. Most of the designers seem to be aware
that if you have to get out of bed to do something then this
destroys any sleepiness you may already have. So provision is
always made for bringing whatever you may want right to you
in bed.

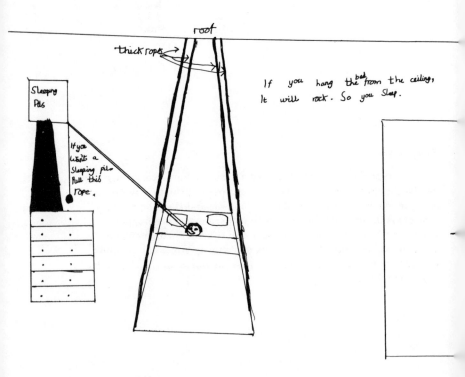

roof

thick ropes →

Sleeping
Pills

If you
want a
Sleeping pill
Pull this
rope.

If you hang the bed from the ceiling,
It will rock. So you Sleep.

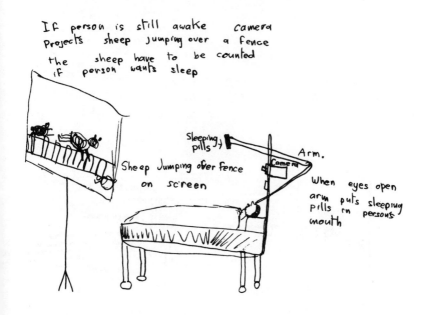

If person is still awake camera
Projects sheep jumping over a fence
the sheep have to be counted
if person wants sleep

Sleeping pills

Sheep Jumping over fence
on screen

Arm.

Camera

When eyes open
arm puts sleeping
Pills in persons
mouth

Sleep – 10

There could be trouble here. A camera projects sheep jumping over
a fence, and the sheep have to be counted if the person wants to
sleep. On the other hand if the person's eyes are open, then an
arm dumps sleeping pills in his mouth. So as long as he is watching
and counting the sheep he is getting a steady supply of sleeping
pills. The reasoning is perfectly sound – either you are awake and
watching the sheep, in which case you need some sleeping pills, or
you are asleep, in which case the sheep are turned off and
everything is as it should be. Unfortunately there is a slight danger
of an overdose, since the sleeping pills would take some time to
act, and if you were a very avid sheep counter you might get a
great number of pills dumped into your mouth.

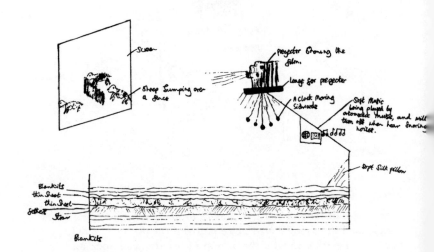

Sleep – 11

Another sheep-counting system, or at least one in which you watch sheep jumping over a fence. As you do this there is a pendulum ticking slowly from side to side to soothe you to sleep. Finally there is soft music which is playing above your head. In many of the previous designs the sleep-making mechanism was turned off in some mechanical manner. In this case, however, the automatic music is turned off by the sound of your snores. Careful attention to the sheets, blankets and pillows to make sure you are very comfortable.

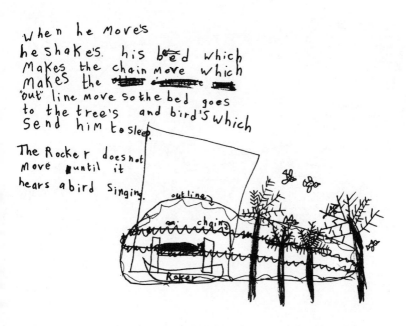

When he moves
he shakes his b̶e̶d̶ which
Makes the chain move which
Makes the ~~other~~ ~~spreader~~ ~~out~~
"out" line move so the bed goes
to the tree's and bird's which
Send him to sleep.

The Rocker does not
Move until it
hears a bird Singing.

outline
chain
Rocker

Sleep – 12

A highly complicated and effective design. Instead of having
'canned' music to make you go to sleep, this time there is the real
thing. Instead of bringing the world into your room you get taken
out into the world. The mechanism is operated by the movement
of the restless non-sleeping person who shakes the bed. This
shaking of the bed makes the chain move, and this chain takes the
bed out into the open air, where birds are singing in the trees. The
singing of the birds puts him to sleep. To enhance the singing of
the birds there is a rocker which rocks the bed. So he lies in bed
being rocked and listening to the sound of the birds. However the
rocker does not get going until it actually hears the birds singing.
An extremely pleasant way of being put to sleep.

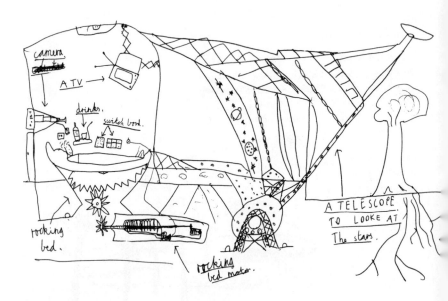

Sleep - 13

This time the entertainment is more indoors although a telescope
is provided to look at the stars. In addition there are drinks,
television and a camera, and a switchboard to let you choose
exactly what you want to do. The rocking mechanism for the bed
is shown in considerable detail. There is a motor with a cog wheel
at the end. This meshes with another cog wheel, which in turn
meshes with a serrated semi-circle on the underside of the bed. So
that as the motor runs first one way, then the other the bed tilts
up fore and aft.

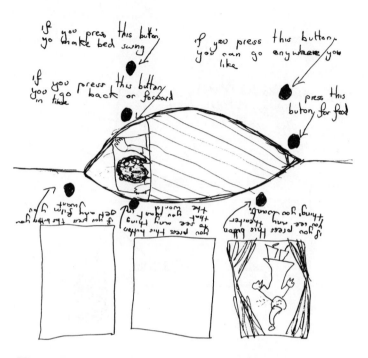

Sleep – 14

The idea of the sleep machine being a sort of entertainment complex, which was hinted at in the previous design, is here carried to its logical conclusion. There are a number of buttons to press, and if you press the right button, you can have virtually anything you want. By pressing the right button you can get any film, or theatre, or food you want. You can also make the bed swing or go backwards and forwards in time. By pressing the right button you can also see anything you want to see in the world or go anywhere you like. In other words this is an automatic dream machine. So while you are still awake you can get anything you want, instead of having to go to sleep and just dream about it. It is not too easy to see why if you were getting whatever you wanted you would wish to go to sleep. Though perhaps this is a better understanding of child psychology than most adults – including myself – have. Perhaps you go to sleep when you are happy and you have everything you want.

gas makes a man
go to sleep. When he's
asleep the gas turns
off itself

←gas

Sleep – 15

A very simple sleep machine which uses gas. The gas puts the man
to sleep, and when he is asleep the gas turns itself off, because if
it didn't turn itself off the man would probably be killed. Unlike
the previous designs this use of gas actually puts the man to sleep
in a very positive way. There is nothing he can do to resist it.
Whereas in the previous designs the idea was to create a setting
which would make it easy for a man to go to sleep, or try to
persuade him to go to sleep. Here he is actually forced to go
to sleep.

Sleep - 16

Another design in which sleep is actually imposed on the person.
It is achieved by the use of sleeping gas which comes out of a
nozzle just above the pillow. But it dosen't seem to matter whether
this is effective or not, because as soon as the head touches the
pillow it operates a lever which releases a weight which drops
down on the head of the person and puts him to sleep. As always
with children, the designer is very practical and knows very well
that if a lead weight hits you on the head it is going to make a
nasty mark, so the weight is covered with foam rubber.

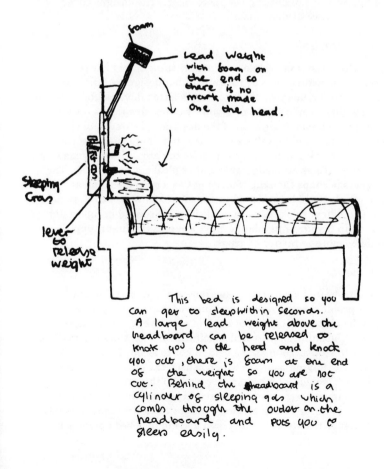

Borrowing

The children treated sleep as something definite that could be
achieved in a definite manner if you used the right apparatus.
Many of the sleep-making devices were borrowed from the adult
world, for instance sleeping pills and drink. Some of the others
appear to have been borrowed from the world of comics, for
instance the weight that thumps you on the head and possibly the
sleeping gas. Some other devices might have been more familiar to
children, for instance the rocking devices and the music/lullabies.
It is perhaps surprising that children should have been so aware
of different ways of putting people to sleep – the designs cover
just about every device in use.

General atmosphere

Some of the designers rely on one single thing to put the person
to sleep, for instance gas or rocking. Other designers however
preferred to include two or more sleep-making devices, for instance
rocking plus sleeping pills, or a voice saying 'sleep' plus rocking,
or gas plus a hammer. Several of the designers, however, did not
seem to be just adding different devices together. They seemed
intent on creating a general sleep-inducing atmosphere by making
the surroundings as comfortable and as pleasant as possible. The
designers perhaps thought of sleep not as a semi-mechanical
state which could be achieved in a mechanical way, but more as
a psychological relaxation. In adult life this second group would
be more in favour of psychotherapy, whereas the first group
would be more in favour of drugs.

Automatic

Children showed a surprising awareness of automatic operations.
In this problem because the operator was putting himself out of
action he obviously could not control all of what was going on.
Many of the children provided specific means for the sleep-making
activity to stop as soon as the person got to sleep. This could be
achieved by having a device which sensed the closing of a person's
eyelids or a device which simply reacted to the sound of his snores.
Other designers were also interested in automatic operation but
this time in automatic operation that got turned on inadvertently.
For instance the weight of a person getting into bed operates a

tape recorder, or else the movement of a very restless person in bed sets off something else, or as the head touches the pillow it activates a lever. All these are very sophisticated uses of control mechanisms, for something is not actually brought about by the intention of the operator but happens when it is triggered off by some other event. There is a big difference between a man switching on a tape recorder before he gets into bed and a tape recorder being switched on automatically by his weight as he does get into bed. Understanding and use of automatic control mechanisms, feedback and feedback cut-off by children shows a surprising grasp of processes that are really quite complicated.

6 Design and Equip a Space Rocket

Design a space rocket in which astronauts could live on the moon for three weeks.

The problem this time is not to achieve a single specific effect, but to furnish a rocket for the three weeks' stay on the moon. It is no longer a matter of being able to find a right answer, but of providing whatever you want. This is a matter of choosing things, choosing some things in preference to others, establishing priorities, finding out what is unnecessary and so on. How would children tackle this problem? Would they carefully assemble the requirements of the astronauts, or would they simply transfer another situation which provided these requirements, and simply install it in the space rocket? On what grounds would children establish priorities? Would they establish priorities in terms of the things that were important to them, or in terms of things that were important to adults or to astronauts? Would they try to imitate what they already knew about space rockets, or would they design their own rockets for use on the moon? The main problem is to provide the living equipment for the rocket on the moon. There is the additional problem that the rocket and the living equipment must take into account the special circumstances of being on the moon. How would children react to this? Would they ignore the fact that the space rocket was on the moon and treat it as though it was on earth, or would they pay a lot of attention to the special circumstances on the moon?

The basic problem is one of deciding what is important, deciding what to put in and deciding what to leave out.

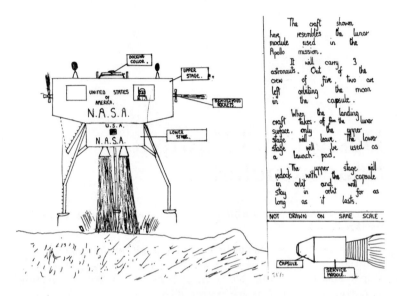

The craft shown here resembles the lunar module used in the Apollo mission.

It will carry 3 astronauts. Out of five, two are left orbiting the moon in the capsule.

When the landing craft takes off from the lunar surface, only the upper stage will leave. The lower stage will be used as a launch-pad.

The upper stage will redock with the capsule in orbit and will stay in orbit for as long as it lasts.

NOT DRAWN ON SAME SCALE.

CAPSULE   SERVICE MODULE.

Rocket - 1

Good drawing of the existing moon-landing vehicle. NASA and the
United States flag are prominent on the sides. Note the docking
collar and the rendezvous rocket (which are functioning in different
directions), and the astronaut in his space suit at the window with
the radio aerial on his back. This is a good example of what might
be called the 'reproduce' type of design, where a child carefully
reproduces what he knows to be the actual state of affairs. Since
children were not specifically asked to design a new space rocket,
the reproduction idiom is perfectly valid and as valid as any more
creative attempts. Being aware of how things are actually done is
just as important as inventing fresh ways of doing them. In this
particular design it is assumed that the existing space capsule can
be internally modified to allow astronauts to live for three weeks on
the moon. There is no reason why this should not be so. We know
that it can support life for a few days and there is no reason why it
should not support life for longer. So here the designer has simply
indicated an existing mechanism which solves the problem. The
designer does not actually go inside the rocket to show the detail of
what is provided and how it functions.

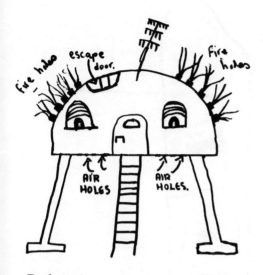

Rocket – 2

Another 'external' design,
showing the outside of the space
rocket. The remarkable
resemblance to the human head
with eyes, nose and hair is
unlikely to be accidental.
Provision of the ladder is
thoughtful, but the air holes
which allow communication with
the outside are probably not such
a good idea. Again the designer
does not go inside the rocket to
show what is provided.

Rocket – 3

This young designer removes the outside of the rocket so that we
can see what is provided inside, and inside are provided all the
essentials for life on the moon, which are simply stated as radio, eat
and sleep. Each of these is delegated to a specific and separate
compartment. 'Eat' is indicated by a table with things on it, and
'sleep' by a bed. The last compartment, although it is unlabelled,
seems to indicate the engine or mechanism. Although simply stated
the idea is comprehensive. Radio is for communication, eat and
sleep are for life support. That is, after all, what the problem
demanded.

Rocket – 4

Another statement of the furnishing of the space rocket. This time it
is so simple as to be laconic. The designer is perhaps a little more
practical than the last designer, because she provides bed, food and
a toilet.

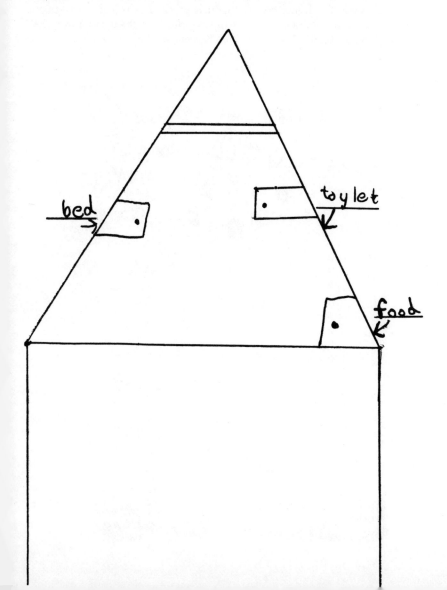

Rocket – 5

In this design the furnishing of the rocket is described in a little more detail. Instead of there just being a label saying 'food' or 'eat', there is a listing of different sorts of food, like meat, cake, bread, special moon sandwiches, and the tablets that are going to be necessary. The living compartment is perched on top of a two-stage rocket, and a lift is used to get the man up from the ground into the top compartment, just as at Cape Kennedy.

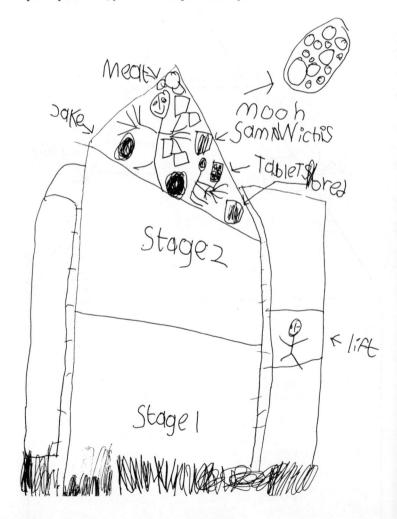

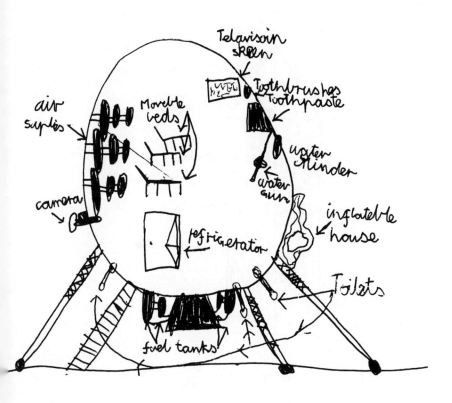

Rocket – 6

Yet more detail, with three movable beds, a television screen, a
refrigerator, camera, water gun, and of course separate
compartments for important things like toothbrushes and
toothpaste. What is important to a child is not necessarily the
same as what is important to an adult. On the side of the vehicle
can be seen a rather useful design, the inflatable house, which
could of course work quite well on the moon, as quite a low air
pressure inside would serve to inflate it. The house might for
instance be used to protect the astronauts, not from the weather,
but from the intense glare of the sun.

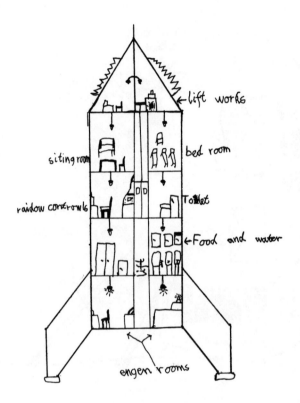

Rocket – 7

This seems to be the doll's house approach. The inside of the space
rocket is furnished just like the inside of a house. Each room is
provided with a lamp and a shade in the middle of the room. It
seems that at the moment only the lights in the engine room are
switched on. The furnishing of the rocket is transferred straight
from the furnishing of a house, so there is a sitting room, a bedroom,
toilet and a room for storing food and water, and other rooms for
radio controls and the engine. Access to the different rooms is
provided by lifts, and the rooms at the top of the rocket seem very
like attic rooms. This is a 'transfer' kind of solution. If people need
houses to live in, then there must be a house inside a space rocket
if they are going to live in it on the moon.

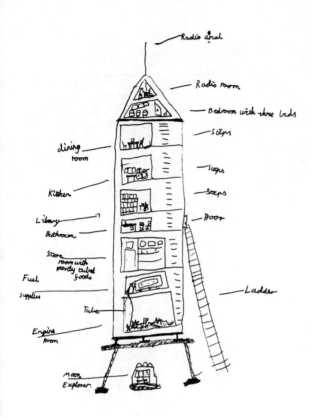

Radio aral.

Radio room

Bedroom with three beds

Steps

dining room

Sugs

Kitchen

Scops

Library

Door

Bathroom

Store room with mostly tubed foods

Fuel supplies

Tube

Ladder

Engine Room

Moon Explorer.

Rocket – 8

Another house with dining room,
kitchen, library, bathroom and so
on. There is, however, an
awareness that this is not an
ordinary house on the surface of
the earth, but a space rocket on
the moon, for in the store room
the food is mostly 'in tubes'.

Rocket – 9

The beds are stacked as bunks. As in most of the designs there are
three beds for three astronauts, because the American space
ventures have usually featured three astronauts. The gas cooker is
carefully provided with the different gas mark numbers. In the
centre of the floor is a mat to make it just like home. An unusual
feature of this particular design is the map of the moon, which is
stuck on the wall so that the astronauts can find their way around.
In this particular drawing there is no attempt to suggest that the
contents are situated within the outer shape of a rocket. The
contents are given directly just as though they were furnishings in a
house, and apart from the map of the moon, there is no indication
that it is a space rocket at all.

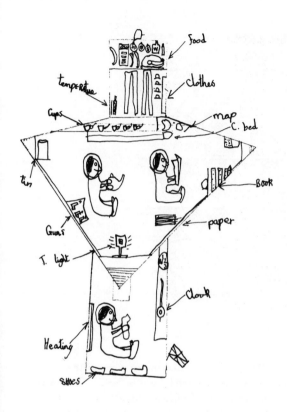

Rocket – 10

This design gets away from the straight 'doll's house' approach, and here the items that are needed are scattered around, for instance a row of cups and some books and also a grandfather clock with a pendulum. On a shelf are three guns, one for each astronaut. The astronauts themselves, wearing their space helmets are sitting down quite comfortably, one of them with a newspaper and the other one apparently about to pour from a teapot. In the food compartment there appears to be a large turkey just ready for serving. At the bottom of the vehicle are three shoes, or more likely, three pairs of shoes, one for each astronaut. A Union Jack is also provided.

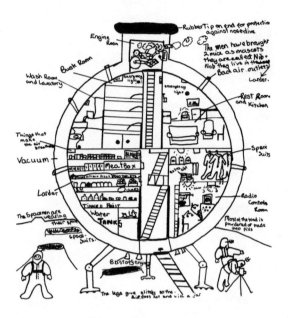

Rocket - 11

In contrast to the simplicity of the furnishing in some of the previous designs, this design shows considerable detail. The larder seems to stock quite a lot of the kind of food you might expect to find in a more earthly larder. On the other hand there is the comment that most of the food is powdered or made into pills. The interior of the rocket is surrounded by a vacuum. There is thus a strange juxtaposition of furnishings which are very directly earthbound and yet a lurking awareness that this is a different situation that calls for a vacuum to retain the heat just as in a thermos flask, and for the food to be powdered or in the form of pills. Two mice have been brought along as mascots, and they can be seen living in the larder alongside the water tank. The spacemen are out of the vehicle wearing their space suits, but obviously they have a spare set of space suits, which can be seen hanging on a rail. There are practical points of detail, for instance all the living rooms are provided with emergency lights, and the whole vehicle itself is provided with a rubber tip on the end as protection against a nose-dive.

Rocket - 12

Most of the designs so far have tried to provide a balanced
environment, in terms of food, sleep, communication and so on, but
some designs seem obsessed with one particular requirement. For
instance in this design, the requirements seem limited to a variety
of food ranging from 'taties' to desserts. These are stocked in sort
of drawers and you can have what you want. When you are not
eating you are sitting strapped in chairs in front of this food panel.
The only additional equipment is a drawer for toilet bags.

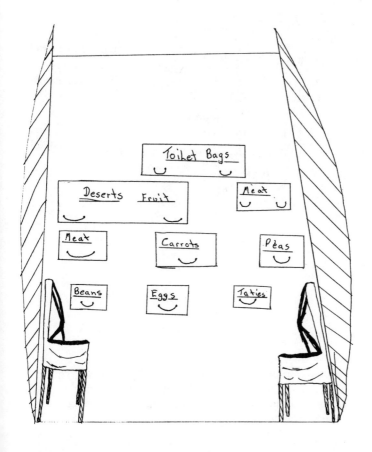

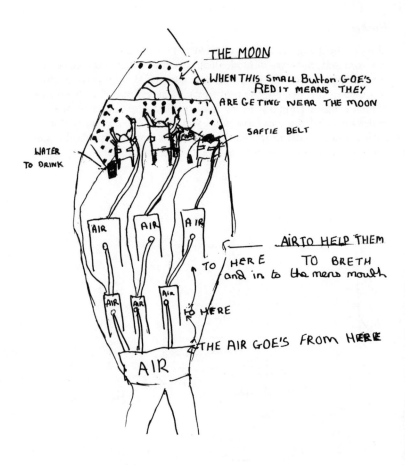

THE MOON

WHEN THIS SMALL Button GOE'S RED IT MEANS THEY ARE GETING NEAR THE MOON

SAFTIE BELT

WATER TO DRINK

AIR   AIR   AIR

AIR TO HELP THEM TO BRETH
TO HERE
and in to the mens mouth

AIR   AIR   AIR

TO HERE

THE AIR GOE'S FROM HERE

AIR

Rocket – 13

This time the concentration is on providing proper air for the three astronauts as they sit in front of a gigantic control panel. The air can be seen to come in from the back and go through the first stage of processing and then on to the second stage of processing before it reaches the astronauts.

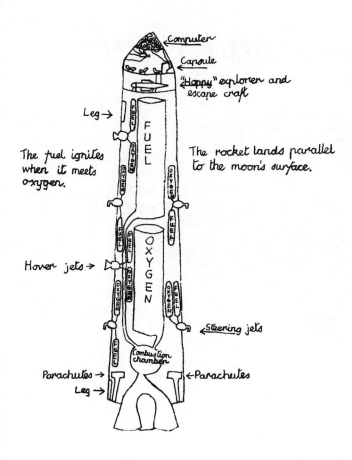

Rocket - 14

Here the concentration is on providing fuel for the motors. Each motor has its own dual chambers of fuel and oxygen. In effect this is a rather realistic view since the actual rockets which go out in space do consist mainly of fuel.

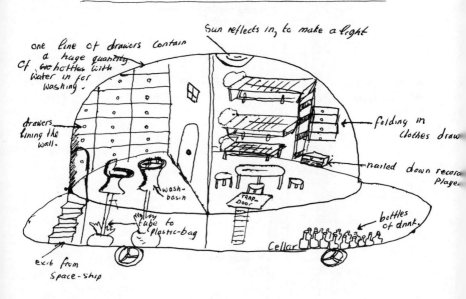

INSIDE OF A SPACE-Rockee

Sun reflects in, to make a light

one line of drawers contain a huge quantity of the bottles with water in for washing.

drawers lining the wall.

folding in clothes draw

nailed down record player.

wash-basin

TRAP-Door

tube to plastic-bag

bottles of drink

Cellar

exit from space-ship

Rocket – 15

Not perhaps a very comprehensive furnishing of space rocket, but
the designer does have an eye for detail. In the roof there is a
reflector so that the sun can make itself into a ceiling light. The
wash basins and toilet are each connected to separate plastic bags,
instead of having tubes just ending in the air below the space
rocket. The record player is nailed down so it can't move about. On
the other hand there is a huge stack of drawers which contain a
quantity of bottles of water just for washing. The overall design
looks a bit like a hat, though it is probably more closely related to a
flying saucer.

Rocket – 16

Another designer with a practical eye for detail. Note how one of
the legs of the rocket is used as the drain for the toilet. There is a
special indoor garden for growing cress. This is really a very
practical idea, and some of the groups working on advanced space
travel are seriously interested in ways of providing food which
actually grows within the space vehicle, instead of just transporting
stored food.

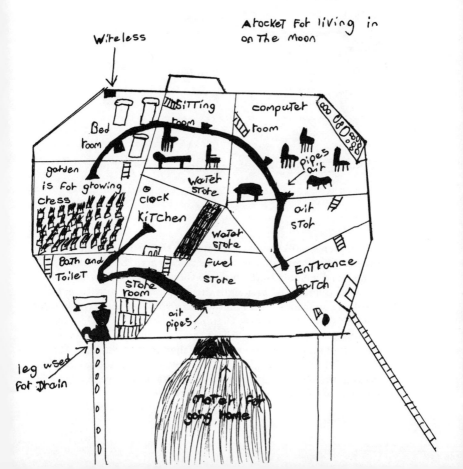

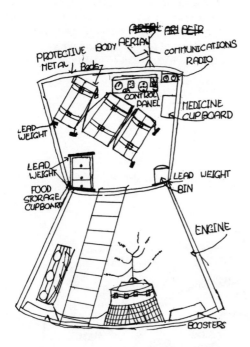

SPACECRAFT

Rocket – 17

This designer is well aware that being on the surface of the moon is not the same as being on the surface of the earth. So she has attached lead weights to the beds, to the storage cupboards, and even to the dustbin. At first sight this might seem a silly idea, for weightless conditions, lead itself would also be weightless. Therefore this might seem less effective than nailing things to the floor as in one of the previous designs. In fact there is a force of gravity on the moon, although it is considerably less than that on earth, so the addition of these lead weights would serve a very practical purpose, in making the objects to which they are attached moveable but much more stable and less likely to be kicked about.

Transfer

Several of the designers simply transferred the idea of a furnished house to the inside of the space rocket, this procedure solved the problem in one go. Because instead of having to try and build up a living environment piece by piece, all that they needed to do was to indicate that the inside of a rocket was like the inside of a house and, as we all know, houses are good places to live in. Transfer, in fact, can also be seen in those designers who simply drew an existing space vehicle, and implied that with this drawing they transferred the full use of that vehicle.

Importance

Where the designers actually built up the living conditions in the space rocket, what features did they consider important? Three things which the designers obviously felt to be the most important were sleep, food and toilet arrangements. The sleeping accommodation was either in the form of a bedroom, or at least in the form of very solid looking beds, one for each astronaut. In real terms this is perhaps a bit surprising because one would imagine that the astronauts would sleep just about anywhere, but it may arise from the fact that with television showing the actual astronauts in their space craft, they are often to be seen in their sort of couches which serve both as seats and as beds. It may also be that sleep is an important part of a child's life. Eating was dealt with both by the provision of a dining room with a full complement of tables and chairs, and also by the provision of rather extensive larders, showing the various sorts of food that were to be consumed. In a design which showed little else carefully listed were meat, bread, cake and moon sandwiches. With the provision of toilets and wash basins one designer even went so far as to provide a huge set of drawers containing bottles of water for washing in.

Apart from these major living considerations various designers included other things they thought to be important, such as a medicine cupboard or first-aid kit, books for entertainment, mascot mice, grandfather clock, mat and so on.

Difference

Many of the designers seem to be torn between trying to provide a living environment such as might be found on earth, and yet being aware that this was the moon, and therefore things would be different. One of them overcame this problem in a simple way, for instance by providing a map of the moon in the room. Others carefully indicated that the food had to be powdered or in tubes, though it looked as though it was very much earth-type food. One designer had a very simple furnished spacecraft, but put each of his astronauts in space helmets to indicate that he was aware that they were indeed in space. A more specific awareness of the problems created by space was shown by the designers who nailed the gramophone to the floor or provided lead weights for keeping the furniture on the floor. On the whole the designers were probably more influenced by experience of real earth shapes than by their ability to design specially for space, for instance beds and chairs look very much like earth-type beds and chairs. It must of course be admitted that the children may only have wished to convey the idea of a chair, and the best way to convey the idea of a chair is to use that shape of a chair which everyone would recognize. If, for instance, you were to invent some very special type of space chair which had no legs, then how would the reader know what you meant? This argument does not really hold up because in several of the designs, the tables and chairs are very carefully labelled as tables and chairs, even if they are unmistakeable.

Improve the Human Body

Draw a picture showing how you could make your body better.

In many of the problems given to the children there was some definite 'end-point' which had to be achieved: weigh an elephant, build a house quickly, invent a sleep machine, etc. This time the problem is open-ended. There is no specific end-point to be achieved just the vague idea of making the body better. The children are left to decide for themselves what improvement they want. Does an improvement consist in being able to do something new that could not have been done before? Or in doing what could be done before faster or more easily?

Our bodies are so familiar that they seem perfect and it is difficult to think how they could be improved. You can improve a design by picking out the obvious faults and correcting them. Another way is to find a gap and fill it. You could also try and add some entirely new function.

Would the children think of an effect they wanted to achieve and then find a way of achieving it? Or would they just make a change for the sake of it and then look around to see what use it could be?

Would the children want to achieve fantastic things like flying to the moon or practical things like getting to school more quickly?

Stephen and I would like a
bigger mouth so we can eat
abit More food at a time.
And we could drink a drop
More

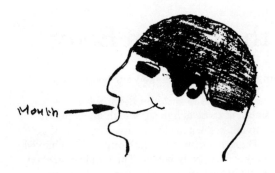

Human design – 1

The improvement consists of a small change in an existing feature
in order to bring about a definite advantage: 'I would like a bigger
mouth so we can eat a bit more food at a time. And we could drink
a drop more.' Someone who had sensibly noticed that when you are
very hungry the mouth is just not big enough.

I would like ears that record what other people said. Then I would not have to go and ask them what they said.

I said, I am going to the Foot ball Mach

Human design - 2

The same designer with another change to give a definite advantage.
The suggestion is that recording a conversation should be a function
of the ear (as in a tape-recorder) rather than of the brain. This is
one of the few design changes that are not accompanied by a visible
alteration in the feature itself (the ear does not change shape or
size).

I think it would be better if my finger's could grow longger and Shorter. Because then I can pick big things up when my finger's are long. And I can pick up Small things when my finge are Small.

Human design – 3

A most excellent improvement to give a definite advantage. A coarse working hand and a fine working hand so people would be just as good at embroidery as at digging ditches.

I would like to change my hair to very pretty hair and so that I could change it short or long when ever I wane to. To save mummy taking me across the road to have a hair cut. And so that if I want long hai badly I can just change it to long hair and to save the money from mummy buying a wig for me to chang my hair.

Human design – 4

The advantage to be gained here is one of money and convenience. The matter is one of real concern to the designer who is after all not asking much. Being able to change appearance at will is not unknown in the animal kingdom (birds with ruffs, etc.).

Human design – 5

More of most things except
fingers and toes. But no reason is
given for this multiplicity and no
advantage claimed.

This is a young man I would like him to have two mouths. 2 noses. 2 eyes. 2 ears 1 neck three arms. 3 legs. 4 or 5 fingers and toes.

Human design – 6

Not just more of the same but direct improvements as well. Spring
feet for a more agile goalie. Expanding-tong-type arms for grabbing
things and people. Supersonic ears. And of course an aerial to call
for help if someone attacks you. Three eyes and noses but only one
mouth, doubled up arms but a third leg. Most children are
inconsistent in the way they multiply up the features and it seems
that aesthetic considerations are just as important as mathematical
or mechanical ones.

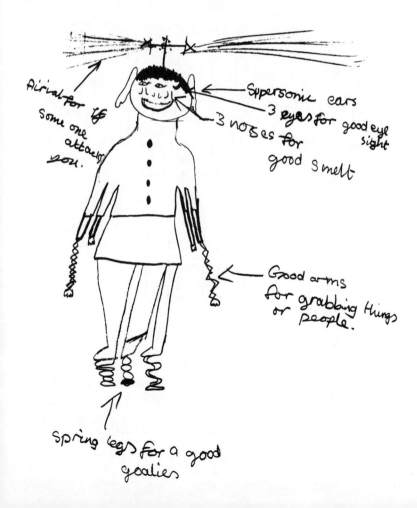

Human design – 7

Another multiplicity example with a rather unexpected and not
entirely convincing reason given: 'so that I could get to school
quicker'.

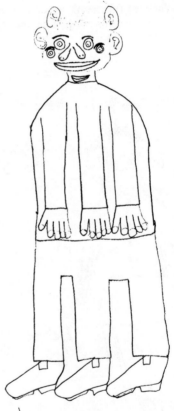

This is a boy these are the thing
that I would like to have 4 eres.
4 eyes 2 noses 2 mouths 3 hands
and arms and 3 legs so that I
could Get to school cwiker.

Human design – 8

Even the dog has benefited from the generous improvement in the human shape. On one side the double arms mean that he can get all the shopping 'in one go'. But on the other side the extra arm is only used to hold an extra lead to the same small dog.

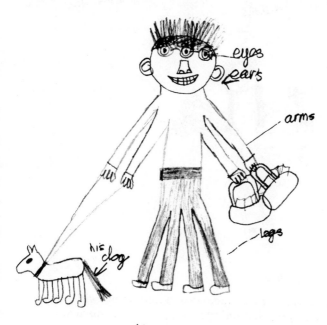

He can get all the shopping in one go

I would like tow more pears of arms so that I can use things more quikkely and to feel more easily. I would like tow on the back and tow on the front and tow on the side. And I would like fiue more fingers on each hand. And my arms. So they can bend back, this will work by praessing a button and the arms will go backwords and forwards

Human design – 9

This time only the arms are increased in number but with octopus-like lavishness: 'press-button' effect suggests mechanized arms rather than natural ones. In time people may indeed come to be fitted with additional mechanical arms. In this case, unlike the previous examples, the multiplicity seems to be for a definite purpose.

This is a Picture of me. I have three eye's becuse if I go blind in one eye I still have two to see with. And I have three leg's becuse if one gets tied I still have two to walk with.

Human design - 10

This time the multiplicity is not to give any special advantage but to provide a 'reserve' capacity. The arms remain unmultiplied suggesting that in this case as well the multiplicity is for a definite purpose.

I would like to have two heads, when I was looking at a book if my other pair of eyes did not like the work they would look at the other page.

Human design - 11

A most unusual design since two heads are usually placed side by side not one above the other like storeys in a house. The designer seems to have a strong sense of duty which requires one head to do what it is told and the other to move on to something more enjoyable.

MY maw has Too pairs
of eys so when one
pair goes to sleep the other
pair wakes up. he has
To mowthes one happy
one sad. he has Two
pairs of arms so when
he gets in to a fight one
pair holds the victim while
The other pair punches.
and he has two pairs
of Legs so is one pair
slip the other pair will
hold him up.

Human design - 12

The reasons given for each additional feature are specific, sane and
practical. A fearsome creature indeed.

Human design – 13

The essence of multiplicity. Just three additional fingers which will
obviously make the owner do her work quicker.

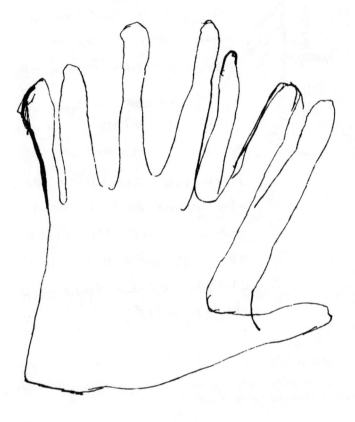

I Would want more fingers on my
hands then I could do my work
quicker

I would Like to
change my nose. I
whant my nose on my
Legs. So that I can
Smell if any bad men
have come that way.
and I the would Like
my nose a very
Strong Smelling nose. and
a very Long nose.
So I can Smell
a Long way Like
a cat.

It will work
when you press a
boton evrething hapens.

Human design – 14

'I would like to change my nose. I want my nose on my legs so that
I can smell if any bad men have come that way and I would like my
nose a very strong smelling nose and a very long nose so that I can
smell a very long way like a cat. It will work when you press a
button everything happens.' A very sensible transposition of the
nose from its useless position up in the air to being near the ground
where all the interesting action is. Note the 'press-button'
mechanism again.

Human design – 15

A combination of both the multiply strategy and the transpose
strategy. Clearly a girl with a strong mind and revolutionary
tendencies. Double ears mean better hearing.

This is a girl with double ears I have
put double ears on her because she will
be able to hear things she
should not hear. and I have
put fingers on her head so. She
can grab anything what is on
a top shelf and her mother
has told her not to get.

Human design – 16

Another design to improve hearing this time by putting the ears on stalks so that they can get closer up to what is being listened to. Naturally these special ears are activated by a button – most things are nowadays (TV, radio, hoover, washing machine, etc.).

I would like to change my ears

I would like to press a button and my ears would shoot out

Then I would not have to strain my ears

I think it would be a good idea.

Button that I press to make ears spring out.

Here

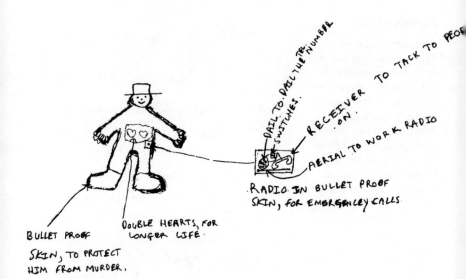

DAIL TO. DAIL THE NUMBER
SWITHES.

RECEIVER TO TACK TO PEOP

AERIAL TO WORK RADIO

RADIO IN BULLET PROOF
SKIN, FOR EMERGENCY CALLS.

BULLET PROOF

SKIN, TO PROTECT
HIM FROM MURDER.

DOUBLE HEARTS, FOR
LONGER LIFE.

Human design – 17

The super-policeman. The child was very concerned about crime, violence and danger, and his design was for the specific purpose of providing better protection. Communication facilities are part of protection. Although the skin is made bullet proof the heart is not and protection is achieved with a spare heart.

Multiply

The simple increase in the number of features is very characteristic of children's attempts to improve the human body. Two sweets are better than one and in general more means better. So more also means faster, easier, stronger and any other advantage you wish. In only a few cases do the additional features have a real reason (one pair of arms to hold the victim and the other to punch him). I have given the same problem to adults and they also favour this multiply strategy more than anything else. Even with sophisticated professional designers more or bigger is supposed to be better (for instance, fins or chrome on American cars).

Transpose

Another simple design strategy used by adults as well as children. Put the eyes in a different place to see better, put the nose near the ground to smell better, put fingers on top of the head to achieve more.

Reason

In most cases it seems that the change in the number of features comes first and it is assumed that the increase is an obvious advantage (if two legs are good three must be better). Even when reasons are given it often seems that they are a sort of rationalizing after the change has been made. This is not unlike much human invention where the design comes first and then you find a use for it. In a few cases there seems to have been a genuine attempt to solve a real problem.

A Bicycle for Postmen

Design a special bicycle for a postman.

It is often thought that children are inventive and original simply because they are ignorant. If you do not know how something is usually done, then you have more chance of coming up with a new way of doing it. Bicycles, however, are very familiar objects to children, and the purpose of giving this problem was to see how children would alter what was already a familiar object in order to make it better.

Problem-solving is quite easy if you are given a definite objective which has to be achieved. Problem-solving is also quite easy if there is some obvious deficiency in a design and you are asked to get rid of that deficiency or fill in some gap. Problem-solving is rather difficult when all you are given is a general idea that you should improve an existing design. This becomes even more difficult when the existing design seems to be a very satisfactory one, as in the case of the bicycle. How would children decide to improve the bicycle? There do not seem to be any obvious deficiences in the design as it has been around such a long time. Nor is it easy to see in what way one could actually improve the design. What could be added to a bicycle to make it better? What could be removed from a bicycle to make it better?

The children were asked to design a special bicycle for a postman, so that their improvements in the bicycle design would be directed to a specific purpose and would not just be general improvements, or change for the sake of change. The child is well aware of the function of a postman. How would he set about re-designing a bicycle in order to let a postman carry out his function more efficiently or more pleasantly?

On what aspects of a postman's function would a child concentrate? Is delivering letters all that there is to a postman's life?

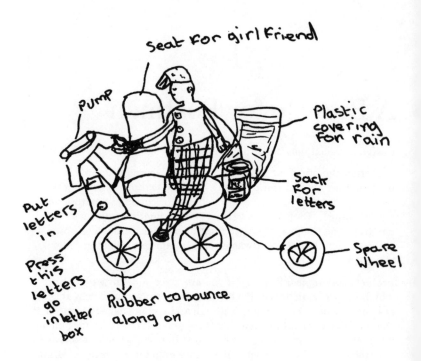

Bicycle – 1

Being a postman is a lonely business because you spend hours all by
yourself riding along. A simple and humane improvement in a
postman's bicycle would be to provide a seat for his girl-friend.
Since it is rather undignified for a girl to sit with her back to the
postman, she can sit side-saddle on the seat which is placed
sideways. Note the spare wheel which is towed along behind in case
of puncture. Note also the clever positioning of the bicycle pump
above the handlebars.

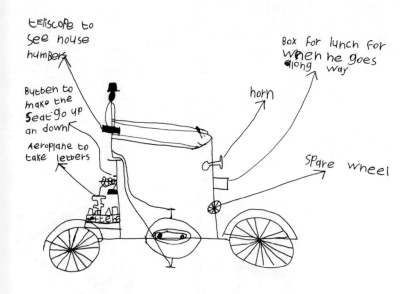

teliscope to
See house
humbers

Box for lunch for
when he goes
along way

horn

Butten to
make the
Seat go up
an down

Aeroplane to
take letters

Spare wheel

Bicycle – 2

Several improvements including the very practical one of a
telescope through which to see small house numbers. Also a button
to make the seat go up and down at a touch, a box for lunch for
when he goes a long way and also a spare wheel. A rather more
exotic touch is the aeroplane that is going to take letters to the
houses and make it unnecessary for him to get down from the bicycle.

Bicycle – 3

A simple change with provision
of letter baskets for him to put
the letters in. These baskets are
rather like the letter baskets that
might be found on an executive's
desk.

Bicycle – 4

At first sight a very ordinary bicycle with 'Sturmey Archer' gears
and a rear-view mirror. But if you look more closely you will find
that there has been a change; it is now a front-wheel-drive bicycle.
There is no indication why the change has been made from back-
wheel drive to front-wheel drive, though of course the front wheel is
very much bigger than the back wheel. At first sight there might
seem to be disadvantages in this design, because the front wheel has
to steer. But in practice, if there did turn out to be any disadvantage
in front-wheel drive, this could be very easily overcome.

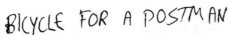

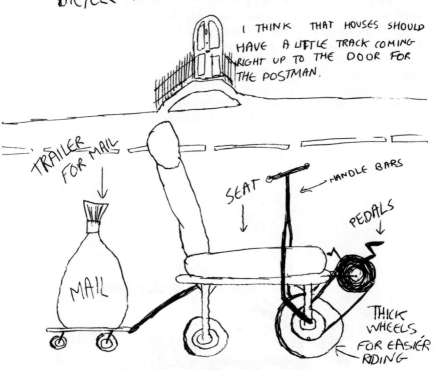

I THINK THAT HOUSES SHOULD HAVE A LITTLE TRACK COMING RIGHT UP TO THE DOOR FOR THE POSTMAN.

TRAILER FOR MAIL

SEAT

HANDLE BARS

PEDALS

MAIL

THICK WHEELS FOR EASIER RIDING

Bicycle – 5

A very sensible designer. He has gone a bit outside his brief in order to suggest that houses should have a little track coming right up to the door so that the postman doesn't have to get down. His design for a bicycle seems most comfortable. It is a sort of armchair bicycle in which you recline back and your feet turn the pedals in the air. This is a good deal more comfortable than having to sit upright with your weight partly supported by the pedals. The wheels are also provided with thick tyres for easy riding. Another innovation is the idea of towing the mail behind on a little trailer. On the whole a design which just looks extremely comfortable.

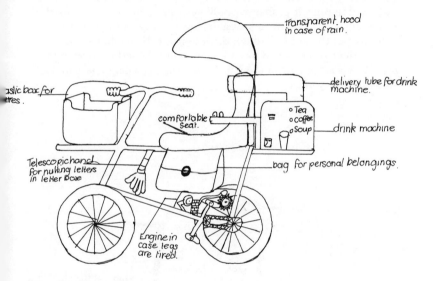

transparent hood
in case of rain.

delivery tube for drink
machine.

o Tea
o coffee
o soup

drink machine

comfortable
seat.

lastic box for
tyres.

Telescopic hand
for putting letters
in letter box

bag for personal belongings.

Engine in
case legs
are tired.

Bicycle - 6

Further refinements such as a transparent hood over the rider so
that he doesn't get wet in the rain, and also a drink machine, where
you put a coin in the slot and then choose whether you are going to
have tea, coffee or soup. To save the postman's energy there is a
telescopic hand for putting letters in letter-boxes. There is also an
engine in case his legs get tired, but if there is going to be an engine
it is hard to see why the postman should not use it all the time. But
perhaps the designer thought that, if the bicycle was motorized
throughout, then it would no longer be a postman's bicycle but a
postman's motorcycle, so the engine is only provided as a sort of
reserve, just as yachts have little reserve engines without ceasing to
be yachts.

Bicycle - 7

This time the motor is definitely described as a secret motor for
going up hills. The idea is that the postman must not be seen to be
using his motor, because that would be cheating, just as if a boat
sculling down the river in the Henley Grand was seen to be using a
motor. Solid rubber tyres are provided in order to stop punctures.
There is a long pole to deliver letters without getting off the bike.
This really is quite a sensible idea. It may appear that this would be
awkward to use – it probably would be at first, but in getting used to
it it might indeed save the postman from getting off the bike to
actually put the letter through the letter-box. He could stop at the
edge of the pavement and use his tong to put the letter through the
box. An essential part of the improved design is a dog-repellant
spray for nasty dogs.

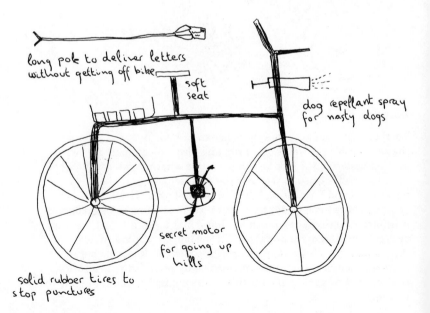

long pole to deliver letters without getting off bike

soft seat

dog repellant spray for nasty dogs

secret motor for going up hills

solid rubber tires to stop punctures

Bicycle – 8

A lot of the designers were very much concerned with the 'nasty-dog' danger to postmen, and they provided a variety of devices to overcome this danger. This particular design provides an instant ghost with which to scare off dogs. The design is not all fantastic, for instance there is a centrally heated sheepskin seat which sounds as if it would be very comfortable. There is also a combined fog and headlamp in one. Wheels have rubber foam tyres to make for extra easy riding, and there are also twenty-four gears, so that there should be no trouble with hills. As in the previous design there is a telescopic arm to drop letters through the box. There is no reason why the instant ghost should not be some sort of inflatable device.

Bicycle – 9

A design to try and make a postman's life very easy by the use of various devices at the end of extendable arms. The dog danger is taken very seriously. One dog is shown being KOed by a punch, another one is seen being attracted first by a joint of meat and then knocked silly by another punch. One gloved arm delivers letters to the letter-box and another one picks up letters which have somehow dropped to the floor. A peculiar innovation provides for attack by badmen. A couple of guns somehow go down underground and then take the gunmen in the rear. The erroneous notice on the handlebars 'No Postman's Leg Left' is supposed to indicate to dogs that there really is no point in pursuing the matter further.

Conventional model: 1970

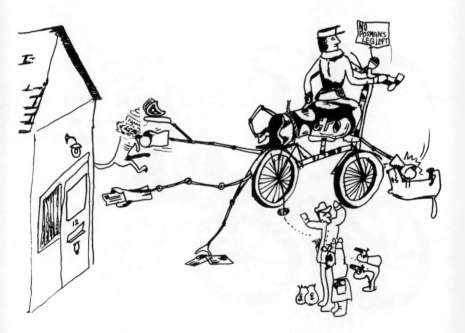

POSTMANS WINTER BICYCLE

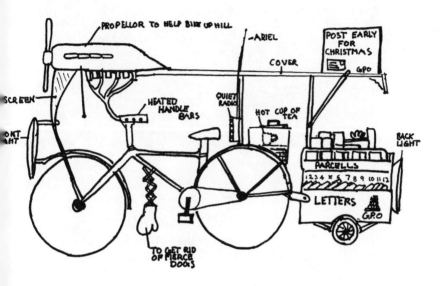

Bicycle – 10

There is provision of an engine and a propellor, but once again this
is only to help get the bicycle up the hill, otherwise the postman is
supposed to pedal in the ordinary way. There is the usual boxing
glove on Lazy-Jane tongs to keep off fierce dogs, and a hot cup of
tea. An interesting innovation is the quiet radio just behind the
postman, so that it can amuse him without upsetting everyone else.
Mail is carried already sorted in a trailer.

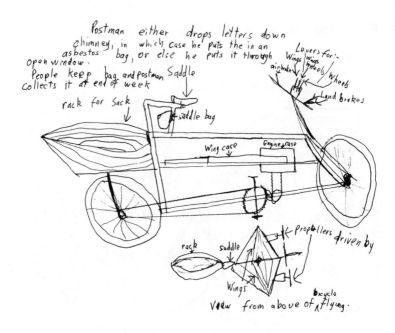

Postman either drops letters down chimney, in which case he puts the in an asbestos bag, or else he puts it through open window.
People keep bag and postman collects it at end of week

Levers for:-
Wings Wings propel Wheels
airbrake Land brakes

rack for Sack

Saddle
saddle bag

Wing case   Engine case

rack   Saddle   Propellers driven by
Wings
View from above of a flying bicycle.

Bicycle - 11

This is a flying bicycle, and the small drawing below shows what happens when the wings are extended. Two small propellers drive the bicycle forward. The designer, however, is a realist and when he recommends that the advantage of a flying bicycle is that you can drop the letter down the chimney, he very carefully specifies that you would have to put them in an asbestos bag, otherwise they would get burnt. An alternative would be to put them in through an open window. The Post Office does not want to go on supplying asbestos bags endlessly. The postman would collect the bags at the end of the week.

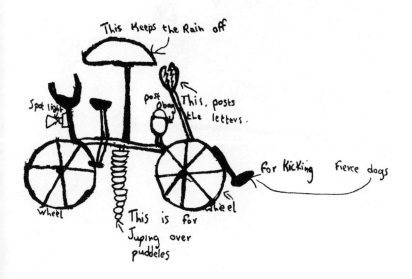

Bicycle - 12

This design is equipped with a device for kicking those fierce dogs
that chase along after a postman's bicycle. An unusual feature of
this particular design is the device for jumping over puddles. So
when you come to a puddle in some way you put down the device
and you sort of pole-vault over the puddles. There is also an
umbrella to stop you from getting wet at the other end.

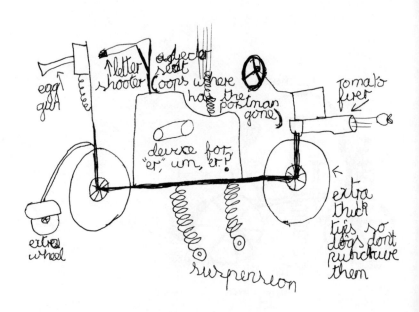

Bicycle – 13

An unusual suspension device reminiscent of the puddle-jumper in
the last design. Instead of having suspension on the wheels
themselves you have two separate wheels on the ends of springs,
which serve to take a lot of weight off the main wheel and
would in fact provide quite a useful smooth ride. There seems to be a
bit of an obsession with springs. There is a tomato firer and egg gun,
a letter shooter and an ejector seat for the postman who has
inadvertently used it (which saves the trouble of having to draw
him). There seems to be a sort of tape-recorder device for uttering
those useful syllables 'er', 'um', 'er', in answer to any questions.

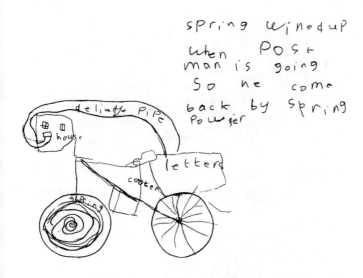

Bicycle – 14

The young designer is very concerned about the postman getting
tired. There is a delivery pipe which takes letters from the bicycle to
the house, but an even more thoughtful provision is the spring on
the front wheel. This spring winds up when the postman is going
out, so that then he can come back by 'spring power'. This is really a
very useful concept. It might not actually work on the basis of
storing energy in the first part of the morning to give it out in the
second part of the morning. But it could certainly work in storing
energy when one has to come to a halt at a house in order to deliver
a letter, and then requires extra energy to get going again. Using
some sort of clutch mechanism the spring would be wound up as you
wished to come to a smooth halt, and then when you got back on
the bicycle you switched the spring back in, and then it gave you a
sharp push off, to save you having to stand on the pedal to get
going. This principle under the more technical sounding name
're-generative braking' is in fact a part of the thinking of advanced
transport groups, who intend to apply something of the sort in the
design of modern buses.

Bicycle - 15

An unusual idea for the quick delivery of letters. You have a metal
stamp on a letter, and then the householder wishing to receive his
letter stands outside with a magnet, and this attracts the letters out
of the postman's bicycle as he goes past. This makes life very easy
for the postman, because all he has to do is to drive past the houses
and it is up to the householders to collect their letters by long-range
magnetism. It seems likely that the letters would get rather mixed
up. On a more sophisticated scale however, magnetic character
recognition is the basis for a lot of cheque sorting in banks.

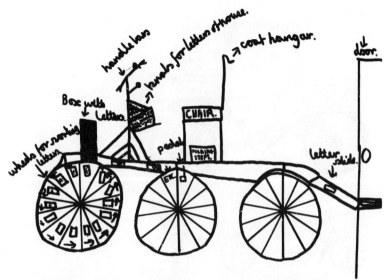

your wheels sort the the letters into alphabetical order, you press the right knobs for the house name + the right letters go down the letter slide + into the house.

Bicycle – 16

The letter-sorting aspect of a postman's job occupies this designer's attention. A special bicycle wheel is provided for sorting the letters, which somehow whizz round in this wheel and then come off it at the appropriate moment and go down a letter slide and end up directly through the letter-box. The postman has a sort of control panel and what he does is to press the appropriate knob. Presumably this operates some sort of scoop mechanism, which scoops the letters off only a certain part of the bicycle wheel. Note the coat hanger behind the seat on which the postman sits.

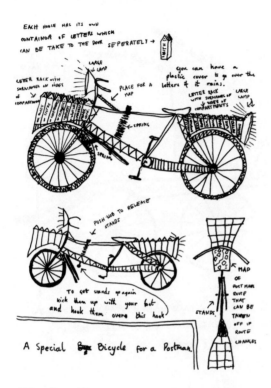

EACH HOUSE HAS ITS OWN
CONTAINOR OF LETTERS WHICH
CAN BE TAKE TO THE DOOR SEPERATELY →

LARGE LAMP

LETTER RACK WITH SURNAMES ON SIDES OF COMPARTMENT

PLACE FOR A MAP

you can have a plastic cover to go over the letters if it rains.

LETTER RACK WITH SURNAMES ON SIDES OF COMPARTMENTS

LARGE LAMP

← SPRING

SPRING

PUSH KNOB TO RELEASE STANDS

MAP OF POST MANS ROUTE THAT CAN BE TAKEN OFF IF ROUTE CHANGES

STANDS

To get stands up again kick them up with your foot and hook them over this hook

A Special ~~Box~~ Bicycle for a Postman.

Bicycle – 17

Further attention to the sorting problem. This time the letters are pre-sorted and placed in little containers, each of which has the appropriate surname on the side. You then take the container to the door, remove the letters, put them through the letter-box and take the container back to the bicycle. In this way you sort out all the letters right from the beginning. A special map stand is provided for the postman, so that if the route is changed he can just put on a new map instead of having to learn it all by heart. The designer has other points which are very practical. For instance, you can pull a plastic cover over the letter racks if it rains. There is also attention to the bicycle stands, because a postman more than anyone else spends all his time getting off the bicycle and trying to prop it up, so he really needs a sort of efficient stand which all bicycles at the moment lack.

Bicycle - 18

A long series of trailers to carry letters and some spare trailers in
case 'there is lots'. Note the special feature of a cushion which is
attached to the bicycle just beneath where the postman sits. This
cushion is carried along with the bicycle so that if the postman has
to get off the bike when it is going fast, instead of landing on the
hard ground he will land on the cushion.

Bicycle – 19

Two major innovations. First of all the postman is not a postman at all but a postwoman. This is not too hard on her because this particular bicycle goes by itself. So efficient is its control system that a newspaper stand is provided so that the postwoman can read the newspapers as she goes on her round. Everything is controlled from the control box.

Bicycle – 20

Automation is carried a stage further here with a full-scale robot with metallic-looking robot hair, who actually drives the bicycle, while the real postman sits behind and controls the robot. A pair of skis are carried on the back and there is an overhead parcel shelf with a multi-tone horn. An interesting provision is the bumper in front of the front wheel. This in fact sounds like quite a good idea, so that when you do run into something, instead of knocking your wheel out of shape you simply absorb the shock with the bumper, which could be very simple and very light.

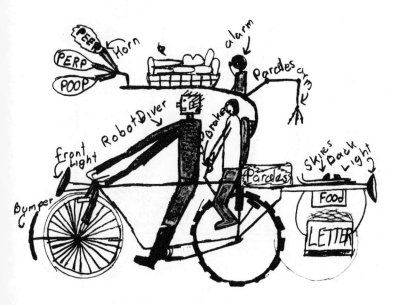

Bicycle - 21

The usual press-button paradise. You press a button and everything
happens. This time there are three buttons. If you press one of them
you will get something to eat. If you press another one you will fly,
and if you press the third button you will get a slave, who
presumably will run and post your letters for you.

The real problem

The children had little difficulty in deciding what were the real
problems in a postman's life. Nasty and vicious dogs were obviously
a very real problem. Getting wet through by the rain was another.
Getting the bike up steep hills was another problem, and even
merited the addition of 'secret engines'. Then of course the postman
might get hungry or thirsty, so it would be as well to provide him
with instant cups of hot tea, or a choice of tea, coffee or soup, and
also some lunch or sandwiches. Postmen have a long way to go and
they could get tired so it might be an idea to try and help them with
engines or by putting a spring on the front wheel. What especially
tired out postmen was having to get down off the bicycle to go and
put letters through the letter-box. To save the postman the trouble
of doing this there were all sorts of devices whereby the postman
could remain in the saddle and then extend a long telescopic arm
which would drop the letters inside the letter-box.

Different solutions

Different designers picked out different problems in a postman's
life. But even when they picked out the same problem they often
adopted completely different ways of overcoming it. For instance
with the real problem of nasty vicious dogs, some designers came
up with the solution of boxing gloves at the end of an extendable
arm which would simply sock the dog. Other designers preferred a
dog-repellant spray, or an instant ghost. This difference of approach
in solving a problem is characteristic of children thinking, and
indicates in a very clear manner that children really do think and
do not simply repeat standard ways of dealing with standard
situations.

Simplicity

Most of the designs seemed a good deal more complicated than the
ordinary postman's bicycle is at the moment. Most of the
improvements consisted of adding some additional feature to the
existing bicycle, and sometimes at the end the bicycle was so
covered with additional features it was hard to discern the original
shape. Children are never as concerned with simplicity, economy
and elegance as adults, because these things have no real meaning
to them. They only have meaning to someone from an aesthetic

point of view, from a cost point of view, or from a design point of view in terms of ease of assembly or maintenance. To a child, effectiveness is much more important than simplicity, and if you have the problem of repelling dogs, then you must have a device to repel dogs, even if it looks ugly or costs more to include. As a general design point it is very difficult to start out looking for simplicity. First of all one looks for effectiveness and completeness, and then when one has got to that stage one tries to slim down the design and look for simplicity and elegance. You can only prune something that is there. If you do not have it there to prune you run the risk of neglecting it entirely.

9 Policemen and Bad Men

If you were a policeman how would you deal with bad men?

Unlike many of the other problems this problem is very remote from a child's life. Children are certainly very aware of policemen, but they are only aware of bad men in an abstract sense. They know bad men exist, but the chance of a child actually seeing a criminal or a criminal being caught or a criminal being tried is very remote indeed. The child's experience of the way policemen deal with bad men or the way bad men ought to be dealt with is derived almost entirely from second-hand sources, such as films, television and comic strips. In these second-hand packaged situations the relationship between bad men and policemen is very prominent, in fact quite out of proportion to its relation in real life. Thus to the child the problem of how to deal with bad men is a real one in terms of his second-hand experience, but a remote one in terms of real-life experience. In tackling the problems would the child just repeat what he knew to be the stereotyped problems from his second-hand experience, or would he do some thinking of his own?

The problem as stated is very open-ended because no indication is given of what particular aspect of dealing with the bad men is intended. Is it a matter of how to catch bad men, or what to do with them when they are caught? In fact the problem is so very open-ended that no particular problem is actually stated. The children are asked how they would deal with bad men if they were policemen. They were not asked to solve the problem of how to catch bad men or to solve the problem of how to make bad men better, or indeed any actual problem. They were simply given a situation and left to deal with it. In tackling the situation, what aims or objective would the children set up for themselves? Would efficiency in catching the bad men be an aim? Would efficiency in punishing the bad men be an aim? Would efficiency in returning the bad men to society be an aim? The ability to define aims, objectives and specifications for oneself may be an essential part of a problem-solving situation. In some problems the aim to be achieved is set out in a very definite fashion, but in other problems there is simply a general situation and within that general situation it is left to the problem-solver to define the problem and to decide for himself what he would regard as a satisfactory solution to that problem. That situation is exactly the case with this particular problem.

There is also the moral aspect of the situation. Are bad men to be regarded as thoroughly bad, or are they to be regarded as bad but improveable. How would the children regard the police – as all powerful and all good, or as relatively human?

Policeman and badman.

rope rofe

Bad men - 1

The problem here has been seen as the basic one of catching the bad
man in the first place. The policeman is the man wearing the
helmet, and he has lassoed the bad man in the age-old fashion. If
you have a bad man the first thing to do is to catch him. Note the
tummy button which is often characteristic of the drawings of quite
young children.

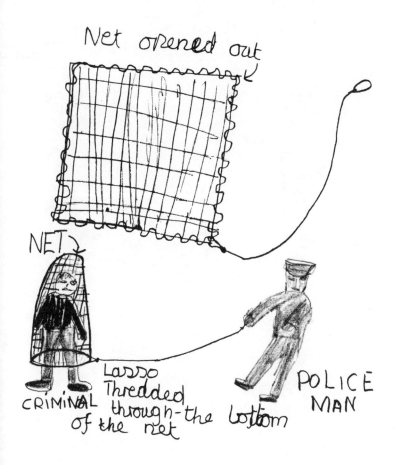

Net opened out

NET

CRIMINAL

Lasso Threaded through the bottom of the net

POLICE MAN

Bad men – 2

Another approach to what might be called the 'mechanical'
approach to catching bad men. A net is thrown over the bad man
and then the lasso at the base is drawn tight. The drawing at the top
shows the net opened out. The policeman in this particular drawing
shows a flat hat, which is extremely unusual, for just about every
drawing shows the policeman in the traditional policeman's
helmet, and this is used as a very strong mark of identification to
show who are the policemen and who are the bad men.

Bad men - 3

This more modern approach to
capture could be called the
'chemical' approach. The
policeman wearing a gas-mask
throws a cannister of gas, which
so upsets the bad man that he
drops both the knife and the
money he is carrying and becomes
immobilized.

use pretty girls as
decoys. Say a gang has ten
members, well ten pretty girls
go off saying "come on" to
each individual member of
the gang, then the girls
walk off in different directions,
and the gang is seperated.
the police then captur the bad
guys who are in a trance.

in trance

Bad men – 4

This approach to capture could be called the 'psychological'
approach. The psychology is subtle and works in two ways. The
first way is to split up the gang by giving each one of them his own
objective, and separating these objectives out so that the gang
splits up as one of them follows one of the ten pretty girls. The
second part of the psychology is that the bad men are so entranced
by the girls that they can lead them anywhere, and in any case the
policeman will have no difficulty in catching them. A strategy that
has proved remarkably effective in capturing bad men, though on the
spy level rather than the petty criminal.

Bad men – 5

What could be called the 'physiological' approach to capture. The
policeman sends the radar-controlled homing leech who injects the
bad men with a paralysing substance. This is rather a fanciful
elaboration of the idea of shooting small darts at wild animals, so
that when the dart pierces the animal's hide it releases a tiny
amount of substance which paralyses and immobilizes the animal
quite painlessly so that it can be captured and in captivity can be
operated on. It seems likely, however, that this particular elaboration
was derived directly from some second-hand source such as a comic
strip. In practice the method seems to have a great number of
advantages. For one thing it is quite harmless so even if the wrong
person got hit by the dart it would not matter because they would
recover without any ill effects. Also it is very much more
satisfactory than gunfire, because gunfire will only immobilize a
man if it hits him in a vital spot, whereas the paralysing dart will
immobilize him if it hits him anywhere at all.

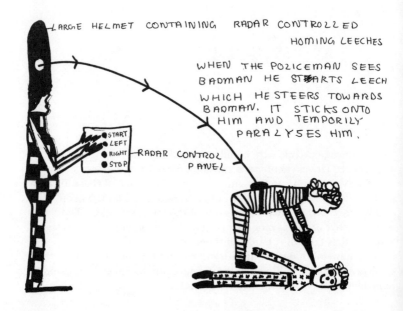

Bad men – 6

We move on now from the
problem of how to catch the bad
man to what to do with the bad
men once they are caught. This
particular design shows the
traditional method of putting the
bad man in prison. The bad man
can be seen behind bars, while
the policeman outside the bars
looks in.

police watch towers ——   —— high wall

Persistent offenders or criminals on life imprisonment are transferred from normal prisons to a special prison town, with shops houses hotels & public services etc but it is all run by criminals who earn wages and do jobs. Police are on watch 24 hours from watch towers and observation posts.

plan

car park   bungalows   garage   pub
                        roads   off town
block of flats   semidetached houses   shops   hotel
                                                    car park
                        gate

Bad men – 7

An extension of the prison concept. Here persistent offenders are kept within a sort of prison town with shops, houses, hotels and public services, all of which are run by the criminals who earn a wage and do jobs. The point here is that criminals are not so much punished as kept apart from society which cannot cope with their inclinations. There is no reason why the prison towns should not be comfortable and efficient, because their main purpose would be to keep the prisoners from the outside, and they would probably serve this purpose better if they were comfortable rather than uncomfortable. The idea is of course that the criminals would stay there for life, not just for a period of punishment.

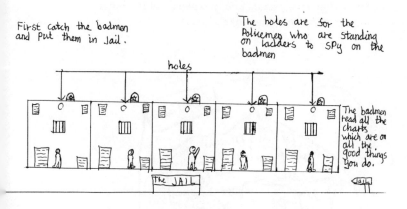

First catch the badmen and Put them in Jail.

The holes are for the Policemen who are standing on ladders to SPy on the badmen

holes

The badmen read all the charts which are on all the good things you do.

The JAIL

The badmen read the charts and come out of Jail as goodmen.

Bad men – 8

A view inside a prison. Five policemen's helmets can be seen as they look through the spyhole to observe what the prisoners are doing inside the cells. The cells are plastered with wall charts which tell you how to be good. It is a bit like the propagandist approach of Red China. People are exhorted to be good by material which is fed to them through their environment. There is no reason to believe that this approach would be totally ineffective.

Bad men – 9

The essence of rehabilitation. The prison as a school that is for making bad men good. In the school can be seen the cells where the bad men live. A large room for physical exercise, because physical exercise is a useful part of rehabilitation. Then there is the school proper and sick bay, dining hall, kitchen and all the other things one might expect in a school. A large wall surrounds the school since it is after all a prison, and in one part of the outer courtyard can be seen the judge's house.

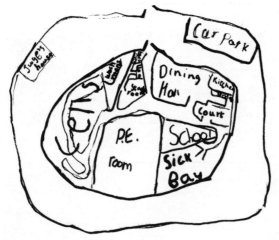

If I was a Police man I would take them to this prison. the school is for making bad men good

Bad men – 10

The 'temptation' approach to rehabilitation. The prisoner is in his
cell with only water, a candle and stale bread. He can look through
a window into a room furnished with a table, chairs, a television
set and wine. He is told he will be allowed a house like this if he
swears not to be a criminal any more. There might of course be
some chance of its working if indeed the criminal was promised
this and could be given this, because it may have been his inability
in the first place to have found this that put him in prison. The
inclusion of wine and a television set as some of the basic goodies
of life is interesting.

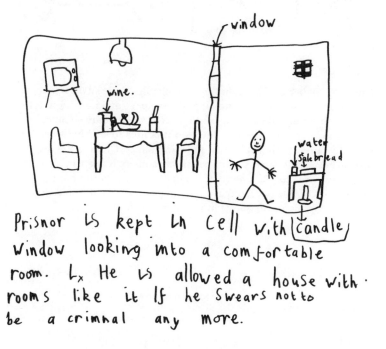

Prisnor is kept in cell with candle
window looking into a comfortable
room. Lx He is allowed a house with
rooms like it If he swears not to
be a crimnal any more.

Bad men – 11

Here the robber is getting better by example. He is sitting
watching a television set showing '*Jackanory*', and he is saying to
himself that he wishes he could do it. When one hears so much
about the harmful effect of television it is nice to see that one child
actually believes that it has an uplifting effect. Outside the prison
are gathered the usual sort of people who make it their business to
discuss what is happening to prisoners, or what should happen to
prisoners. On this occasion at least they seem to be decided that the
particular prisoner in question is being reformed.

Bad men – 12

Here rehabilitation is on the direct hypnotic basis. The policeman
is hypnotizing the bad man and putting him to sleep, and when he is
asleep suggesting to him that he will never commit another crime.
It is interesting to speculate that if the hypnotic method was
effective whether society would in fact approve of it, or whether it
would be termed 'brain-washing'.

Screen showing crime film

Film projector

Receiving hammer on head every time a crime is shown. This makes him connect crime with pain and so stops him committing it.

Badman

Policeman operating hammer box

Bad men – 13

This time the therapy is more orthodox behaviour therapy and is what might be called aversion therapy. The criminal is being shown a crime film and there is a policeman operating a hammer box, so that when a crime is shown on the screen, the policeman drops the hammer on to the head of the bad man. In time the idea is that the pain of the hammer blow would be associated with crime and thereafter the criminal will be less inclined to commit the crime. Orthodox aversion therapy would probably use an electric shock instead of a hammer, but otherwise the principle is exactly the same.

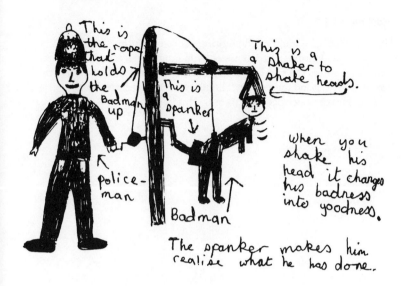

Bad men – 14

This time the bad man is being shaken and spanked on a special
machine. The purpose of this shaking and spanking is not
apparently punishment, nor is it a version of behaviour therapy, the
idea is simply to make the criminal realize what he has done. There
is also a claim that when you shake a bad man's head it changes it
automatically from badness into goodness. It is interesting to
speculate how society would react to some sort of physical
mechanical method (perhaps even brain surgery) to change bad men
into good men.

Bad men – 15

Here instead of a good head-shaking there is another method of
making the criminal good. This is by means of electrical impulses,
which are imparted to his head as he sits in a chair. These electric
impulses are 'good medicine'. The machine is operated by a
policeman who is concerned to make him good.

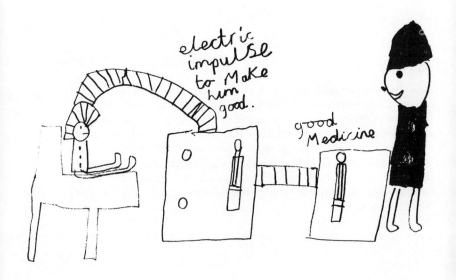

Bad men – 16

This particular design does seem to be concerned with punishment, or at any rate with trying to make life extremely uncomfortable for the prisoner. There is a robot (complete with plug into an electric wall socket), whose job it is to shout 'bleep-bleep' and to clobber the man from time to time. There is a very large pair of pinchers with which to pinch him, a duster to tickle his toes, and a 'thing to pull his hair'. In addition there is a lever which comes down on the bad man's head and a special machine which pops balloons just behind him. In short this is a collection of all the most unpleasant things that a child can conceive of. Although it must be admitted that most of the unpleasant things are more uncomfortable than physically harmful.

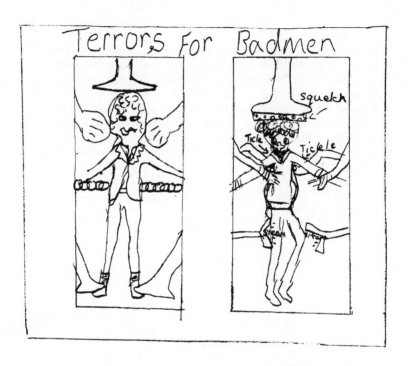

Bad men – 17

Another discomfort machine. In one of the chambers a bad man is
punched and kicked and knocked on the top of his head. In a
second chamber he is treated rather as a car might be treated in a
car-wash. There is a squelching thing that comes down on his head,
and then all sorts of tickling arms which tickle him; as in a car-
wash jets of steam come out at about the height of his knees.

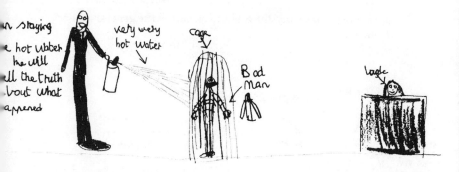

Bad men – 18

This time the discomfort verges on torture. The bad man is held in a cage and then he is sprayed with 'very, very hot water', so that he will tell the truth about what has happened. The function of the lady sitting at the desk in the corner is not quite clear.

Bad men – 19

More punishment. The policeman starts off by hitting the bad man over the head with a truncheon and giving him a headache. He is then taken to prison, and while in prison there is a big stone which continually comes down on top of the bad man's head and hurts him. Like some of the previous examples there is no actual indication of what this treatment is supposed to acheive. Then it may not be supposed to achieve anything, but to be part of the general idea of punishment.

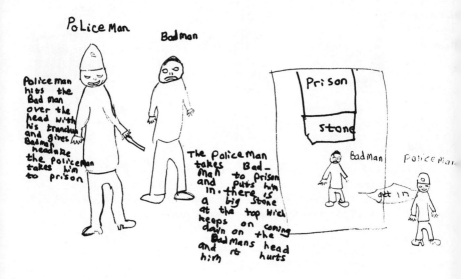

Bad men – 20

A no-nonsense, uncompromising approach to the treatment of bad
men. They are taken up by police in what appears to be an RAF
plane and then simply dropped into the sea somewhere. In that
somewhere sea sharks' fins appear to be numerous. Dealing with
bad men in this particular case seems to be disposing of bad men in
as direct a way as possible.

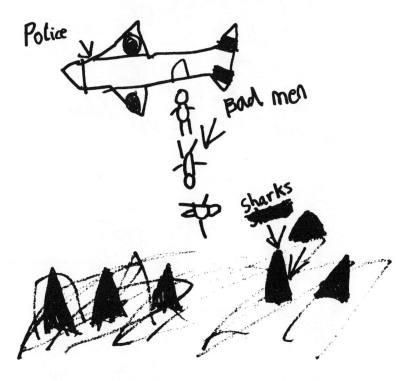

Bad men – 21

In this solution to the problem the two opposite attitudes to bad
men are summarized very neatly. You take them to the 'head
dealer' for a chat. The head dealer is clearly the psychiatrist. That
is to give them pyschotherapy or to rehabilitate them in any other
way. The alternative is quite simply to hang them.

Bad men – 22

This design is completely different to the preceding ones. All the preceding designs were concerned with catching criminals and then with how to treat them in prison. This particular idea is concerned not with catching criminals but with catching motorists. There is a mechanism of lines and lights on the road and under the car. And what happens is that if the car goes across the lines at more than the regulation speed, then the lights flash. This is a highly ingenious and highly practical system. It would be very easy to have lines buried just under the road surface so spaced that if you cross them at more than a certain speed a light would flash and this would instantly reveal that you were above the speed limit, and your car could then be stopped by the police.

The lights and the lines jerk it if it is over the speed limit it is a machanism under the car and on the road

Identification

It seems likely that all the children were not tackling the same problems. Some of the children seemed to be tackling bad men in the sense of nursery naughtiness, which could be put right by being put in an uncomfortable situation, such as having balloons popped behind your head or your feet being tickled with a duster. Other children seem to be dealing with the stereotype of the criminal as dealt with in the cartoon strip – even to the extent of hurling him out of an aeroplane into shark-infested waters.

Change

While some of the designers seemed to accept that criminals would always be criminals and that the only way to treat them was to keep them separate from society or punish them, others felt that somehow it would be possible to make a bad man into a good man. This could be achieved either by dissuasion, or temptation, or more likely by some purely physical means such as electric impulses or aversion therapy by means of hammer blows to the head.

Pure image

Throughout the designers accepted that the policemen were on the side of the good and were always good, and that the baddies were always bad. Both the police and criminals had pure images, in black and white on either side of the fence. It might be interesting to see whether this same effect would hold in other countries. It may be peculiar to the regard in which the English police system is held, or it may arise directly from second-hand experience (TV, cartoon strips, etc.) in which the policemen are indeed always good. It is interesting that no distinction was made between policeman whose job it was to catch the criminals, and the prison system whose job it is to look after the prisoners, or to reform them. Catching the criminals and dealing with them after capture was assumed to be entirely the responsibility of the police force.

No trial

The way the problem was worded gave the impression that the men who were being dealt with were already classified as 'bad men'. This is probably why none of the designs showed any trial process in which the bad man was actually proved to be a bad man. This was more likely to be a fault in the problem wording which pre-judged the issue, rather than to any lack of interest in justice on the part of the children. In second-hand experience (comics, TV, films) the bad men are of course so classified as bad men because one can look in on them as they go about their bad activities. One can see them committing crimes and plotting crimes, so that in the mind of the viewer there never is any doubt that a bad man is a bad man.